BOOK BY BOOK

Book by Book

NOTES ON READING AND LIFE

MICHAEL DIRDA

HENRY HOLT AND COMPANY   NEW YORK

Henry Holt and Company, LLC
Publishers since 1866
175 Fifth Avenue
New York, New York 10010
www.henryholt.com

Library of Congress Cataloging-in-Publication Data

Dirda, Michael.
    Book by book : notes on reading and life / Michael Dirda.—1st ed.
        p. cm.
    ISBN-13: 978-0-8050-7877-0
    ISBN-10: 0-8050-7877-0
    1. Books and reading. 2. Dirda, Michael—Books and reading. 3. Best books.
4. Reading—Social aspects. 5. Commonplace-books. I. Title.
Z1003.D575 2006
028.9—dc22   2005055451

First Edition 2006

Illustrations © Elvis Swift

Printed in the United States of America
1   3   5   7   9   10   8   6   4   2

To Oberlin College

The main interest in life and work is to become someone else that you were not in the beginning. If you knew when you began a book what you would say at the end, do you think that you would have the courage to write it? What is true for writing and for a love relationship is true also for life. The game is worthwhile insofar as we don't know what will be the end.

—MICHEL FOUCAULT

CONTENTS

Preface

AT HOME IN THE WORLD

Live-and-let-live over stand-or-die, high spirits over low, . . . love over charity, irreplaceable over interchangeable, divergence over concurrence, principle over interest, people over principle.

— MARVIN MUDRICK

Over the past fifty years I've spent a lot of time—some might say an inordinate amount of time—in the company of books. Storytelling has always enchanted me, and early on I found myself reading just about anything that came my way, from Green Lantern comics to the great classics of world literature. My memoir, *An Open Book*, recounts a young life unexpectedly shaped by this omnivorous and indiscriminate reading. After childhood, though, I ceased being a purely "amateur" reader, only to become a professional one, first as a graduate student in comparative literature, and since 1978 as a professional reviewer and columnist for the *Washington Post Book World*.

During these past three decades the *Post* has kindly allowed me to write about nearly any sort of book that caught my fancy, and my fancy can be quite promiscuous—ancient classics one week, science fiction and fantasy the next. Despite all these hours of turning pages, I don't view myself as a bookworm, one of those bald-pated Daumier scarecrows peering through bottle-top spectacles at some tattered, leather-bound volume. There's more to life than reading. I've also fallen in love and married, spent Saturdays ferrying noisy offspring to soccer games, mowed grass, folded laundry, and suffered my share of what Shakespeare called "the thousand natural shocks that flesh is heir to."

A normal enough life, then. Yet even as a kid back in working-class Lorain, Ohio, I decided that what I wanted most of all was—how shall I put this?—to feel at home in the world, which meant to know something of the best that has been thought, believed, and created by the great minds of the past and present.

In some ways, that ambition must sound odd, even slightly romantic. But let me explain. About the age of twelve or thirteen, I grew enamored of the story of the Count of Monte Cristo. Suave, cosmopolitan, wealthy, charismatic, the count actually starts life as a naive young sailor named Edmond Dantès, betrayed by those he trusted and imprisoned on the Château d'If for a crime he never committed. At first he despairs. But one day he hears a quiet scraping noise coming from inside his cell wall—tunneling—and in due course meets the learned Abbé Faria, who eventually teaches him everything an accomplished man of the world should know. The young sailor studies, practices, learns, remembers. And so when, after many years, he is finally able to escape and seek a reckoning with those who wronged him, Edmond Dantès has transformed himself into the urbane and accomplished Count of Monte Cristo.

Alexandre Dumas's novel remains a great parable about the power of learning and education and calls to mind one of our most fundamental American convictions: that any of us may, through hard work, fashion a new and better life for himself. As Henry David Thoreau long ago observed, "If a man advances confidently in the direction of his dreams and endeavors to live the life which he has imagined, he will meet with a success unexpected in common hours."

In childhood and early youth most of us naturally read for escape, pleasure, and inspiration; as young adults we use our school texts to learn a profession or trade; and then as full-fledged grown-ups we add yet another, perhaps deeper purpose to our reading: We turn to books in the hope of better understanding our selves and better engaging with the meaning of our experiences. Let me say, right off, that I believe a work of art is primarily concerned with the creation of beauty, whether through words, colors, shapes, sounds, or movement. But it is impossible to read serious novels, poetry, essays, and biographies without also growing convinced that they gradually enlarge our minds, refine our spirits, make us more sensitive and understanding. In this way, the humanities encourage the development of our own humanity. They are instruments of self-exploration.

For *Book by Book*, I've set down some of what I've learned about life from my reading. In its character the result is a florilegium: a "bouquet" of insightful or provocative quotations from favorite authors, surrounded by some of my own observations, several lists, the occasional anecdote, and a series of mini-essays on aspects of life, love, work, education, art, the self, death. There's even, occasionally, a bit of out-and-out advice.

Though my emphasis clearly remains on books as life-teachers, readers searching for any definitive answers or gurulike pronouncements won't find them here. Soon enough one learns that there are no straightforward solutions to most of life's perplexities. Great fiction, in particular, eschews the reductionist and obviously didactic, instead reveling in complication, pointing out options, at most revealing the consequences of one course of action over another. Contradiction, not consistency, second thoughts, rather than dogmatic certitude, lie at the heart of humane understanding, and all those who try to simplify experience usually only succeed in narrowing it. To my mind, life should be complex, packed with questioning, full of misdirection and wasted effort—a certain number of mistakes is, after all, the price for "living large." Arthur Schnabel remains the nonpareil interpreter of Beethoven's piano sonatas, yet he made occasional fumbles in his fingering. But to play such music as it should be played required the pianist to push himself to his limits. Schnabel's motto was that of all great souls: "Safety last."

As I assembled these pages, my intention was to produce a book that could stand, however sheepishly, on the same shelf as Cyril Connolly's *The Unquiet Grave*, Robertson Davies's *A Voice from the Attic*, and W. H. Auden's *A Certain World*. Above all, I hope the result is, to echo the poet Horace's old formula, *dulce et utile*—enjoyable and useful—a book to read slowly, to browse in, and return to.

For just this reason you might want to keep a pencil nearby to mark favorite quotations or to scribble in the margins and on the endpapers. These are the sort of pages that demand to be "personalized," amplified, and enriched with your own reflections, made uniquely yours. Perhaps *Book by Book* may even encourage you to start creating a reader's guide of your own.

N.B.—Some of the authors cited use the generic "man" or the pronoun "he" to refer to the totality of humankind. The female half of the population will, I trust, make allowances for this largely outmoded convention.

Quotations are usually identified simply by author; uncredited material is my own.

BOOK BY BOOK

One

LIFE LINES

Much of *Book by Book* has been gleaned from a small notebook into which I have copied striking quotations and passages from my reading. Such volumes are typically called commonplace books, though their contents tend to be anything but commonplace. What follows are a number of general axioms about life, a few well known and some contradictory, but all of them worth carrying around in your head for their insight, solace, and counsel.

Character is fate.—Heracleitus

A man that is born falls into a dream like a man who falls into the sea.—Joseph Conrad

There is no such thing as perpetual tranquility of mind, while we live here; because life itself is but motion, and can never be without desire, nor without fear, no more than without sense. —Thomas Hobbes

Remember that every life is a special problem, which is not yours but another's; and content yourself with the terrible algebra of your own.—Henry James

What others criticize you for, cultivate: It is you.—Jean Cocteau

Where is your Self to be found? Always in the deepest enchantment that you have experienced.—Hugo von Hofmannsthal

The point is to . . . live one's life in the full complexity of what one is, which is something much darker, more contradictory, more of a maelstrom of impulses and passions, of cruelty, ecstasy, and madness, than is apparent to the civilized being who glides on the surface and fits smoothly into the world.—Thomas Nagel (summarizing the teaching of Friedrich Nietzsche)

To enjoy yourself and make others enjoy themselves, without harming yourself or any other, that, to my mind, is the whole of ethics.—Sébastien-Roch-Nicolas de Chamfort

Life is to be fortified by many friendships. To love, and to be loved, is the greatest happiness of existence.—Sydney Smith

Every day one should at least hear one little song, read one good poem, see one fine painting and—if at all possible—speak a few sensible words.—Johann Wolfgang von Goethe

People must never be humiliated—that is the chief thing.
—Anton Chekhov

Our main business is not to see what lies dimly at a distance, but to do what lies clearly at hand.—Thomas Carlyle

There is only one line to be adopted in opposition to all tricks: that is the steady straight line of duty, tempered by forbearance, levity, and good nature.—Duke of Wellington

The tragedy of being both rational and animal seems to consist in having to choose between duty and desire rather than in making any particular choice.—Mortimer J. Adler

It is a good lesson for a man to step outside the narrow circle in which his claims are recognized, and to find how utterly devoid of significance, beyond that circle, is all he achieves, all he aims at.
—Nathaniel Hawthorne

We are always getting ready to live, but never living.
—Ralph Waldo Emerson

In life, I have learned, there is always worse to come.
—Julian Maclaren-Ross

Who speaks of victory? To endure is everything.
—Rainer Maria Rilke

Lives devoted to Beauty seldom end well.—Kenneth Clark

Two

THE PLEASURES OF LEARNING

Some people will never learn anything, for this reason, because they understand everything too soon. —ALEXANDER POPE

THE START OF SOMETHING BIG

For many grown-ups, long past the age of scissors and coloring books, September provokes a familiar frisson. Something in our cortex sparks to the memory of Big Chief tablets, three-ring binders, stiff leather shoes, scratchy clothes. Come September the past is mentally recaptured, and we are again second or seventh or twelfth graders. A new teacher, a strange desk, different classmates await. This year we will learn cursive or algebra, study Greek mythology or physics, read *Bread and Jam for*

Frances, take the SATs. We will also keep journals and suffer through gym class, deliver oral book reports, and debate whether the United States should withdraw from the United Nations. Many of us will naturally try out for the class play or just miss being elected to the student council or fall hopelessly in love again or get into a fight on the blacktop, not far from the swing sets and the old teeter-totter, where we skinned our knees.

Some fall mornings such unspoken, almost unthought memories just barely break the dulled surface of our adult minds; perhaps only when we glimpse little kids waiting for yellow buses, or hear the distant, muffled brass of a high school marching band practicing on a brisk Saturday afternoon. And the joy of learning? Yes, for a week or two in those early Septembers, we might feel eager, even downright industrious; but then the steady grind of homework would inevitably turn us back into our normal sullen selves, again fearful of the pop quiz, terrified that we would be called on next to go up to the blackboard, frantic in our attempts, always vain, to remember the formula for calculating the area of a parallellogram or the spelling of "supercilious."

THE POINT OF IT ALL

The aim of education is "to develop in the body and in the soul all the beauty and all the perfection of which they are capable."—Plato

The first object of education is to teach the young mind to foster the seeds of piety, the next to love and learn the liberal arts, the third to prepare itself for the duties of life, the fourth, from its earliest years, to cultivate civil manners.—Desiderius Erasmus

Charles Fourier "believed that the aim of education was not to impart a body of knowledge or to wash children free of sin, but rather to make it possible for them to discover and express their true natures."—Francis Beeding

We call the higher education that part of human training which is devoted specifically and peculiarly into bringing the man into the fullest and roundest development of his powers as a human being.—W. E. B. DuBois

To "rouse and stimulate the love of mental adventure . . . To give this joy, in a greater or less measure, to all who are capable of it, is the supreme end for which education of the mind is to be valued."—Bertrand Russell

The development of the faculty of attention forms the real object and almost the sole interest of studies. . . . Attention consists of suspending our thought, leaving it detached, empty, and ready to be penetrated by the object; it means holding in our mind, within reach of this thought, but on a lower level and not in contact with it, the diverse knowledge we have acquired, which we are forced to make use of.—Simone Weil

The preconditions for learning should include "habits of attention to what others are saying, the ability to keep quiet and wait one's turn in discussion, courtesy in response."—Alan Ryan

The primary function of education is to make one maladjusted to ordinary society.—Northrop Frye

A school should be the most beautiful place in every town and village—so beautiful that the punishment for undutiful children should be that they should be debarred from going to school the following day.—Oscar Wilde

THE KNOWLEDGE MOST WORTH HAVING

"Once in a class of graduate students," recalled the distinguished Canadian novelist Robertson Davies, "I met a young man who did not know who Noah was."

What should a person know of the world's literature? It has always seemed obvious to me that the great patterning works ought to lie at the heart of any structured reading program. By "patterning works" I mean those that later authors regularly build on, allude to, work against. There aren't that many of these key books, and they aren't all obvious classics. Here's a roughly chronological short list of those that the diligent might read through in a year or two. For such famous works you can hardly go wrong with any good modern editions, though for the Bible the Authorized, or

King James, Version is the one that has most influenced the diction and imagery of English prose.

The Bible (Old and New Testament)
Bulfinch's Mythology (or any other accounts of the Greek, Roman, and Norse myths)
Homer, *The Iliad* and *The Odyssey*
Plutarch, *Lives of the Noble Grecians and Romans*
Dante, *Inferno*
The Arabian Nights
Thomas Malory, *Le Morte D'Arthur* (tales of King Arthur and his knights)
Shakespeare's major plays, especially *Hamlet, Henry IV, Part One, King Lear, A Midsummer Night's Dream*, and *The Tempest*
Cervantes, *Don Quixote*
Daniel Defoe, *Robinson Crusoe*
Jonathan Swift, *Gulliver's Travels*
The fairy tales of the Brothers Grimm and Hans Christian Andersen
Any substantial collection of the world's major folktales
Jane Austen, *Pride and Prejudice*
Lewis Carroll, *Alice in Wonderland*
Arthur Conan Doyle, *The Adventures of Sherlock Holmes*

Know these well, and nearly all of world literature will be an open book to you.

CLASSROOM REPORTS

The high-school English teacher will be fulfilling his responsibility if he furnishes the student a guided opportunity, through the best writing of the past, to come, in time, to an understanding of the best writing of the present. He will teach literature, not social studies or little lessons in democracy or the customs of many lands. And if the student finds that this is not to his taste? Well, that is regrettable. Most regrettable. His taste should not be consulted; it is being formed.—Flannery O'Connor

The "elective system" is "the democratic principle of admitting all subjects as of equal educational value." In the end, this has always "resulted for the lazy in the search for what was not hard, and for the industrious in the search for what they could do best."—E. K. Rand

I have never worked in a coal mine or a uranium mine, or in a herring trawler; but I know from experience that working in a bank from 9:15 to 5:30, and once in four weeks the whole of Saturday, with two weeks' holiday a year, was a rest cure compared to teaching in a school.—T. S. Eliot

There is, on the whole, nothing on earth intended for innocent people so horrible as a school. To begin with, it is a prison. But it is in some respects more cruel than a prison. In a prison, for instance, you are not forced to read books written by the warders and the governor (who of course would not be warders and governors if they could write readable books) and beaten or otherwise tormented if you cannot remember their utterly unmemorable contents. In the prison you are not forced to sit listening to turnkeys discoursing without charm or interest on subjects that they don't understand and don't care about, and are therefore incapable of making you understand or care about. In a prison they may torture your body, but they do not torture your brains. . . .

Moreover, at school students are "taught lying, dishonorable submission to tyranny, dirty jokes, a blasphemous habit of treating love and maternity as obscene jokes, hopelessness, evasion, derision, cowardice, and all the blackguards' shifts by which the coward intimidates other cowards."—Bernard Shaw

Our culture tends "to regard the mere energy of impulse as being in every mental and moral way equivalent and even superior to defined intention." Instead we should consider "an idea that once was salient in western culture: the idea of 'making a life,' by which was meant conceiving human existence, one's own or another's, as if it were a work of art upon which one might pass judgment. . . . This desire to fashion, to shape, a self and a life has all but gone from a contemporary culture whose emphasis, paradoxically enough, is so much on self."—Lionel Trilling

Within the contemporary university various groups advocate retreat into provincialisms of ethnicity, gender, sexual orientation,

or some other form of communitarian identity. These exclusionist tendencies stand in direct opposition to literal learning. They constitute the xenophobic mentality of the small town. . . . They champion the world of village athletes, smug in their neighborhoods, never testing themselves against the big league teams.
—Frank M. Turner

Schools reek with puerile nonsense. Their programmes of study sound like the fantastic inventions of comedians gone insane.
—H. L. Mencken

The truth is that much of American education aims, simply and brazenly, to turn out experts who are not intellectuals or men of culture at all: and when such men go into the service of government or business or the universities themselves, they do not suddenly become intellectuals.—Richard Hofstadter

Those who are slow to know suppose that slowness is the essence of knowledge.—Nietzsche

IN WILDNESS IS THE PRESERVATION OF THE WORLD

Humankind, noted the dour T. S. Eliot, cannot bear very much reality. One way people avoid it is to imagine a time when society was truly courtly, genteel, or comradely. If only we could, say, reinspire our children with noble ideals, they—never us parents—

could build again a golden age and become its heroes, light-bringers, Nobel laureates. (We do tend to forget, as the poet Randall Jarrell quipped, that the people who lived in a golden age probably went around complaining how yellow everything was.)

The matter of ideals lies at the heart of education: What, finally, are the values we wish to impart? In some compendia of moral wisdom—such as William Bennett's *Book of Virtues*—we are bludgeoned with powerful accounts of good and evil, where virtue is nearly always triumphant. To endure times of crisis and doubt, we are told, people require strong, clear lessons, with unambiguous moral points. This is pure Aristotle, by the way, who felt that virtuous behavior was largely the product of habit and practice.

Certainly, such an approach will create a citizenry assured of itself, anchored in its convictions. Yet do we want a nation of true believers? Moralists tend to promulgate creeds of rationalism, individual self-discipline, faith—all the sturdy yeoman traits. But what of ecstasy, community, and doubt? Surely, as the poet Yeats said, body should not be bruised to pleasure soul. Ought our schools to produce young fogeys, ten-year-old saints and cautious teenagers who never jaywalk or drive too fast? Civility and courtesy are crucially important, yet, deep down, Americans seldom demonstrate any high regard for an obedient Little Lord Fauntleroy or Goody Two-shoes. Our heroes don't follow the rules; they flout them. We admire rebels, mavericks, drifters, scoundrels, and outcasts. The most archetypal Americans are, after all, Huckleberry Finn, Scarlett O'Hara, Malcolm X, and Bart

Simpson. We need to learn from them as well as from noble George Washington and Clara Barton.

In short, if you are given lined paper, write crosswise. At least occasionally.

WHAT GOOD TEACHERS DO

True education always starts by granting some kind of initial authority to the teacher, for ultimately, in the words of the theological historian Robert Wilken, we learn best by placing our "confidence in men and women whose examples invite us to love what they love."

In Saint Augustine's *On Christian Doctrine*—a short treatise on the nature of reading and intepretation—the church father declares that the path to appreciating a book or writer should always begin with love. This notion isn't strictly Christian, however. It lies at the heart of nearly all education in antiquity, for then the student looked to his teacher, to his patriotic ancestors, and to the great heroes of the past as models for the sort of man he might become. The classicist William Arrowsmith insists that such emulation should remain central to learning: "The teacher is both the end and the sanction of the education he gives. This is why it is completely reasonable that a student should expect a classicist to live classically. The man who teaches Shakespeare or Homer runs the supreme risk. This is surely as it should be. Charisma in a teacher is not a mystery or nimbus of personality, but radiant exemplification to which the student contributes a correspondingly radiant hunger for becoming."

Little wonder that William Arrowsmith's favorite play was Sophocles' *Philoctetes* and his favorite scene that in which Philoctetes allows the young Neoptolemus to hold the bow of Heracles. For Arrowsmith this sacerdotal moment represents the handing on of the heroic ideal—and is an emblem of the proper function of education.

Throughout history the exemplary teacher has never been just an instructor in a subject; he is nearly always its living advertisement. Socrates or Alfred North Whitehead, Diotima or Albert Einstein, each represents the learning he or she expounds. Writing of the critic and teacher John Crowe Ransom, the poet Anthony Hecht recalled that "Mr. Ransom did not lecture, he inquired, and he invited the class to join his inquiry. . . . For one learned from him, not facts or positions, but a posture of the mind and spirit, a humanity and courtesy, a manly considerateness that inhabited his work as it did his person."

Character, then, counts. The famous nineteenth-century master of Balliol, Benjamin Jowett, consistently advocated the delight of hard work. "The object of reading for the Schools," he said, "is not primarily to obtain a first class [degree], but to elevate and strengthen the character for life." To a lazy student he added, "You are a fool. You must be sick of idling. . . . But the class matters nothing. What does matter is the sense of power which comes from steady working." No lesson, in or out of the classroom, is more important than that one. The patient accretion of knowledge, the focusing of all one's energies on some problem in history or science, the dogged pursuit of excellence of whatever kind—these are right and proper ideals for life. Only by loving fiercely can we hope to be rewarded; only through such intensity do we make ourselves worthy of what we love.

Yet like God, teachers sometimes move in mysterous ways their wonders to perform. Consider the opposing examples of the no-nonsense classicist Maurice Bowra and Richard Cobb, a historian of modern France. Of Bowra, the cultural historian Noel Annan writes, "He would approach the Michelangelo Holy Family, pause, regard it as if it were a recalcitrant colleague, deliver judgement, 'Greatest work of man,' and plod along to the next." Of Cobb, his student Colin Jones says that "undergraduates . . . told of tutorials spent with him variously asleep, drunk, talking for hours about Georges Simenon and other favoured French novelists, or going down on all fours and barking like a dog. His teaching life was interspersed with wild carousing, scandalous behaviour, perpetual spats with the Master of his college; he was thrown out of more hotels and bars than any Oxford professor of history before (and even since)." Certainly both these eminent scholars lived up to what the philosopher George Santayana whimsically described as the chief function of dons: "to expound a few classic documents, and to hand down as large and pleasant a store as possible of academic habits, maxims, and anecdotes."

Above all, though, teachers and mentors should never let rules constrict their humanity. So insists Samuel Pickering, the model for the English teacher in the film *Dead Poets Society*, "To educate for the future, one must educate for the moment. Classes should sprawl beyond particular subjects. In digressions lie lessons.

Expose students to possibilities. Let them know about your fondness for china, birds, tag sales, and gardening. Talk to them about economics and sociology, to be sure, but also about places you have been and things you have seen and thought. Instill the awareness that for the interested person days and nights glitter."

LEARNING ON YOUR OWN

Nowadays our "self-help books" tend to concentrate on the soul; they teach us how to be happier with the people we are; they urge us to make friends with our inner or spiritual self, sometimes even with our inner child. But in the not-so-distant past "self-help" meant self-education, while "education" usually meant memorization and rote learning. You didn't learn in order to feel better about yourself; you (crassly) learned how to make people think the better of you. An extensive vocabulary, an "educated" accent, the mastery of rhetorical skills, a ready fund of poetry and snappy anecdotes—these sorts of attainments would convey to prospective employers or possible mates that the speaker was accomplished, intelligent, and personable. To those who could talk well, the world was waiting to listen. Or so implied books like Wilfred Funk's *Thirty Days to a More Powerful Vocabulary* and Dale Carnegie's *How to Win Friends and Influence People* or his *Quick and Easy Way to Effective Speaking*.

Such rhetorical "surface" learning was even then frequently dismissed as merely a veneer of social grace and smooth talk covering an opportunistic, even slightly shady purpose. Hadn't Samuel

Johnson summed up Lord Chesterfield's similarly worldly and didactic letters to his son as teaching the morals of a whore and the manners of a dancing master? Nonetheless, a boy or girl could learn about the beauty of language and the power of words from the vocabulary-builder Funk, and if you studied the Carnegie manual diligently, you could give a speech people would pay heed to. Moreover, all the self-help mahatmas urged their acolytes to read the Bible for its prose, to memorize famous poems and Abraham Lincoln's Gettysburg Address, to practice reciting the speeches of Hamlet and Rosalind, Portia and Prospero.

Ultimately, these manuals underscored the esteem still attached to erudition. By stressing how to acquire the appearance of deep and extensive learning, they implicitly taught the importance of the real thing. But our values have altered: Today, anybody with a fair knowledge of world literature and history is commonly regarded as a kind of innocent fool or harmless fuddy-duddy. To possess humanistic learning, once widely aspired to, often seems elitist, unimportant, or simply eccentric. Who would be a scholarly E. R. Curtius or earnest Hannah Arendt in the edgy age of Microsoft? Quote a verse from the Bible or a line from William Wordsworth, mention the date of a battle or a character out of Charles Dickens, and expect to be regarded with a mixture of awe and suspicion. Erudition makes people feel uneasy; at worst it can seem vaguely undemocratic. Better to talk about last night's episode of the latest sitcom, something we can all enjoy equally.

Or is it?

Long ago, Aristotle proclaimed that all men and women desire to know. We instinctively want to learn things. In essence, this is what makes us who we are, distinct from the other animals around us. And it is this passion that brings us our deepest happiness. To gain new knowledge of the world, the past, and our selves, to understand our place in the universe or discover the laws that govern it, these are the activities of human beings at their best. Most humanistic learning, however, builds on the achievements of the past. For instance, all Western philosophy has been called—by Alfred North Whitehead—a series of footnotes to Plato. But if you don't know Plato, the footnotes will make little sense. In Santayana's much repeated aphorism, those who cannot remember the past are condemned to repeat it. Worse still, those who don't remember where they've been will soon find themselves utterly lost. Men and women who read and study and learn may go temporarily astray, but they can never be completely lost. Knowledge isn't only its own reward; it gives us maps through the wilderness, instruments to guide our progress, and the confidence that no matter where we are we will always be, fundamentally, at home.

TELLING TALES OUT OF SCHOOL:

Novels about school life have been popular for generations—think of Thomas Hughes's *Tom Brown's Schooldays* or James Hilton's *Goodbye, Mr. Chips*. Here, again in roughly chronological order, are some more contemporary classics about teachers and students. They tend to be either very funny and satirical or deeply moving and inspiring, reflective, perhaps, of the Janus-like character of education.

Evelyn Waugh, *Decline and Fall*
Mary McCarthy, *The Groves of Academe*
Muriel Spark, *The Prime of Miss Jean Brodie*
Kingsley Amis, *Lucky Jim*
John Williams, *Stoner*
Vladimir Nabokov, *Pnin*
Michael Campbell, *Lord Dismiss Us*
John Knowles, *A Separate Peace*
Randall Jarrell, *Pictures from an Institution*
John Updike, *The Centaur*
John Barth, *Giles Goat-Boy*
David Lodge, *Small World*
Malcolm Bradbury, *The History Man*
Alexander Theroux, *Darconville's Cat*
Harry Allard and James Marshall, *Miss Nelson Is Missing!*
Francine Prose, *Blue Angel*
James Hynes, *The Lecturer's Tale*
Richard Russo, *Straight Man*

And just a handful of stories, memoirs, and plays:

Saki, "The Schwartz-Metterclune Method"
Jesse Stuart, *The Thread That Runs So True*
George Orwell, "Such, Such Were the Joys"
Cyril Connolly, "A Georgian Boyhood" in *Enemies of Promise*
Lionel Trilling, "Of That Time, Of That Place"
Bernard Malamud, "A Summer's Reading"
Ronald Harwood, "The Browning Version"

HUMANE SOCIETY

Every child should be taught what used to be called the social graces: good manners, clear speech, the art of dinner-table conversation, sketching, singing, competence in playing a musical instrument, and even ballroom dancing. Upon such simple foundations as these, true civilizations are built.

Certainly I've come to believe that educated men and women should be—take a deep breath—tolerant, courteous, acquainted with the world's history, art, and literature, knowledgeable of modern science, "concerned" and active citizens, thoughtful about philosophical and religious questions, able to express strongly held views with clarity and force, devoted to family, and conscientious in the performance of their work.

That said, many of the world's artists and visionaries, overreachers and revolutionaries—the people who aim to improve society, enlarge our imaginations, or win our battles—will be anything but ladies and gentlemen. (In the stark wisdom of Horace Walpole: "No great country was ever saved by good men because good men will not go the length that may be necessary.") Obsession has its place, and our lives would be the poorer without our saints and superstars. Still, moderate character traits—temperance, studiousness, deliberation, appropriateness, prudence—should provide the ground for general civilized behavior. The cardinal virtues offer a bulwark against the temptations of fanaticism, whether in the form of religious zealotry or political jingoism, ruthless ambition or mindless conformity. As the Victorian poet William Cory neatly wrote, one of the underappreciated benefits of education is that it "enables you to express assent or dissent in graduated terms." Sometimes we may need to violate these mild, humane precepts, sometimes we do need to fight, but our reasons had better be good ones and subject to periodic reevaluation. Picasso, who could draw with the grace and beauty of line of a Renaissance master, knew perfectly well the rules he might choose to violate.

"Become who you are" went an ancient adage. Learning should lead to an independence of mind built on solid knowledge and a capacity for critical thinking. Unfortunately, ours is a society where doing well on examinations and standardized tests has grown so overemphasized that we have forgotten the importance for a young person to simply flounder about, try out various daydreams, make and learn from mistakes. "It is a rule of God's Providence," said John Henry Newman, "that we succeed by failure." Certainly the motto for any school, for any student of whatever age, should be Samuel Beckett's noble paradox: "Try again. Fail again. Fail better."

Three

WORK AND LEISURE

No one who lives in the sunlight makes a failure of his life.

—ALBERT CAMUS

SLOWING DOWN

Long ago Henry David Thoreau observed—in probably his most famous single sentence—that "the mass of men lead lives of quiet desperation." Certainly a sense of alienation, of being disconnected from our truest selves, of having somehow lost our way is now so common that many of us simply take it for granted. It's the human condition, the fault of original sin, the fallout from a consumerist culture, or the result of a narcissistic preoccupation with our own egos.

Lying awake at 2 A.M., though, even the most apparently successful among us might wonder: Did I somehow take the wrong turn in the road? What went wrong? How did I come to be so dissatisfied with everything? A good deal of this malaise can be blamed on the American cult of speed. We are always on deadline, rushing from one appointment to the next, grabbing a quick bite at our desks, constantly multitasking, repeatedly checking our personal digital assistants and e-mail, weeping with road rage when the traffic slows, logging in ten or twelve hours at work, day after day. "No time to say hello, goodbye," sang out Disney's cartoon White Rabbit. "I'm late, I'm late, I'm late."

How many of us live on that edge, that fraying edge? In every aspect of our daily routines we feel overbooked, overscheduled, and overextended. "The cost of a thing," also wrote Thoreau, "is that which I call life, which is required to be exchanged for it immediately or in the long run."

A hundred years ago, the great polymath William Morris confessed, "Apart from the desire to produce beautiful things, the leading passion of my life has been and is hatred of modern civilization." The poet–political activist–designer frankly loathed "the swinish luxury of the rich" and, perhaps more surprisingly, thought no better of the middle classes: "It is their ambition and the end of their whole lives to gain, if not for themselves yet at least for their children, the proud position of being obvious burdens on the community." When imagining the human future, he even prophesied our own shoddy world of computers and concrete: "Was it all to end in a counting-house on the top of a cinder heap?"

In polemics like "How We Live and How We Might Live" and "Useful Work versus Useless Toil," Morris blasts "the puffery of wares, which has now got to such a pitch that there are many things which cost far more to sell than they do to make." But what, then, is true wealth? "Wealth is what Nature gives us and what a reasonable man can make out of the gifts of Nature for his reasonable use. The sunlight, the fresh air, the unspoiled face of the earth, food, raiment, and housing necessary and decent; the storing up of knowledge of all kinds, and the power of disseminating it; means of free communication between man and man; works of art, the beauty which man creates when he is most a man, most aspiring and thoughtful—all things which serve the pleasure of people, free, manly, and uncorrupted. This is wealth."

Throughout his writings, Morris hammers away at the simple point that "the chief source of art is man's pleasure in his daily necessary work, which expresses itself and is embodied in that work itself." "Have nothing in your house," he also pleads, "that you do not know to be useful, or believe to be beautiful." Once called in by a duke to offer his views on the furnishings in the nobleman's palatial home, Morris suggested burning everything in it on a huge bonfire.

VOCATION/VACATION

An unfulfilled vocation drains the color from a man's entire existence.—Honoré de Balzac

We succeed in enterprises which demand the positive qualities we possess, but we excel in those which can also make use of our defects.—Alexis de Tocqueville

So long as men praise you, you can only be sure that you are not yet on your own true path but on someone else's.—Friedrich Nietzsche

Consider the person who lets frivolities dominate him completely, until he becomes quite beside himself with all his pointless amusements and stupid crazes; such an individual may believe himself to be living happily, but the more he is convinced that this is so, the more desperately miserable his existence really is. —Cicero

It was not by gentle sweetness and womanly self-abnegation that she had brought order out of chaos; it was by strict method, by stern discipline, by rigid attention to detail; by ceaseless labor, by the fixed determination of an indomitable will.—Lytton Strachey (describing Florence Nightingale)

One's greatest pleasures are derived from the uneducated part of one's personality.—Johann Wolfgang von Goethe

An 1890s decadent once met a young girl, of about twenty, "with a lithe body like a snake, a great red dangerous mouth, and enormous dark amber eyes that half shut and then expanded like great poisonous flowers. 'Nuffing amuses me,' she said, with her curious childish lisp, 'everyfing bores me. Nuffing ever did amuse me. I have nuffing to amuse me, nobody to be amused with. I don't care for men, women's talk always bores me. What am I to do? I don't know what to do with myself. All I care for is to sleep. Tell me what is there that will give me a new sensation?' And she lay back, and gazed at me through her half-shut lids. I bent down and whispered, 'Opium.' "—Arthur Symons

We refilled our glasses with cognac, after which all things seemed possible.—William Gerhardie

The natural flights of the human mind are not from pleasure to pleasure, but from hope to hope.—Samuel Johnson

It's odd how soon one comes to look on every minute as wasted that is given to earning one's salary.—P. G. Wodehouse

The maturity of man—that means, to have reacquired the seriousness that one had as a child at play.—Friedrich Nietzsche

If a thing is worth doing, it is worth doing badly.—G. K. Chesterton

It should not be forgotten how much the loser contributes to almost any game.—Lord Dunsany

The universal demand for happiness and the widespread unhappiness in our society (and these are but two sides of the same coin) are among the most persuasive signs that we have begun to live in a labor society which lacks enough laboring to keep it contented. For only the animal *laborans* and neither the craftsman nor the man of action, has ever demanded to be "happy" or thought that mortal man could be happy.—Hannah Arendt

Sunday, July 19, slept, awoke, slept, awoke, miserable life.
—Franz Kafka

Work is the best, and a certain numbness, a merciful numbness.
—D. H. Lawrence

TO WORK IS TO PRAY

How should one spend a day? Or a lifetime? In truth, how we divide up work and leisure is a far more vexing question than it might initially seem. Work, for instance, can be of two major kinds: that which we like to do and that which we must do. Leisure, similarly, can restore our minds, spirits, and bodies, or it can sap those same minds, spirits, and bodies.

As with exercise and lovemaking, what matters in proper work is intensity. Generate enough intensity long enough, and you pass "into the zone," "the sweet spot," "the flow." After dogged effort there suddenly descends a pervasive sense of what is almost grace, transcendence, an inner nonchalance. Everything simply falls into place without effort, as though we were—temporarily—a gifted natural athlete or creative genius. After all, Mozart never needed to agonize over whether he was setting down the right notes: Whatever notes he set down were bound to be the right ones. This is genius, yes. But something similar arises with those who have studied, persisted, and broken through.

Goethe insisted that "no blessing is equal to the blessing of work. Only lifelong work entitles a man to say: I have lived." Similarly, Balzac asserted that constant, steady work was the law of both life and art. The great French novelist would labor through the night, fueled by cup after cup of coffee, writing the first drafts of his *Comédie Humaine*, then spend much of the day—after a brief nap—correcting, amplifying, and reworking the printer's proofs of his books somewhat farther along in the publishing process. (There is a thrilling description of Balzac's work habits—and his work habit, too, for he took to wearing a monk's robe at his desk—in Stefan Zweig's old, slightly romanticized biography, *Balzac*.) No surprise that such a demiurge died at fifty-two, from drinking—it was said—fifty thousand cups of coffee, though overwork, lack of exercise, and an impressive girth doubtless played their parts too.

When nothing matters but to realize their vision, writers and artists often tend to become such dynamos of intensely focused energy. Stendhal produced *La Chartreuse de Parme*, a peak of French fiction, in just fifty-three days; the perfectionist Gustave Flaubert would worry his sentences day after day, spending hours deciding whether to use a comma or a semicolon; Marcel Proust hardly left his cork-lined room once he'd plunged into his "search for lost time." Some imaginations only seem to kick in when their possessors bring to bear almost supernal fervor. An awed interviewer once exclaimed to the jazz saxophonist Charlie Parker, "You do amazing things on the saxophone, Mr. Parker." The musician replied, "I don't know about amazing—I practiced for fifteen hours a day for a few years." Centuries earlier Michelangelo complained that people wouldn't be so astonished at his sculpture if they knew how hard he'd had to labor to achieve his mastery.

The point is: You generally can't wait for inspiration, so just get on with the work. Discplined, regular effort will elicit inspiration, no matter what your field.

Anthony Trollope didn't write quite as much as Balzac, but he was hardly a slouch, producing nearly fifty novels, and mostly thick Victorian novels at that. For Trollope a writer is a man (or woman) who makes his way to a desk each morning and . . . writes. Before heading off to his regular, full-time job as an administrator for the British postal system, Trollope awoke at 5:30, day after day, drank a cup of coffee, and sat down before a quire of paper, pen in hand:

> All those I think who have lived as literary men,—working daily as literary labourers—will agree with me that three hours a day will produce as much as a man ought to write. But then, he should have so trained himself that he shall be able to work continuously during those three hours—so have tutored his mind that it shall not be necessary for him to sit nibbling his pen, and gazing at the wall before him, till he shall have found the words with which he wants to express his ideas. It had at this time become my custom . . . to write with my watch before me, and to require from myself 250 words every quarter of an hour.

So nearly every twenty-four hours—even when traveling (to Egypt, the West Indies, Australia)—Trollope produced on average 3,000 words.

Before beginning a project, he prepared a diary in which he calculated the number of weeks the book would require, then each day he entered the number of pages written. With this system, he explained, "if at any time I have slipped into idleness for a day or two, the record of that idleness has been there, staring me in the face, and demanding of me increased labour, so that the deficiency might be supplied." Trollope was that admirable and rare phenomenon, an absolute professional. "In the bargain I have made with publishers . . . I have prided myself on completing my work exactly within the proposed dimensions. But I have prided myself especially on completing it within the proposed time,— and I have always done so."

W. H. Auden said that a poet must keep hidden his passion for his shop, Evelyn Waugh that even revision and the correcting of publisher's proofs must be done con amore. The flamboyant genius Colette adopted as her writing motto *"La règle guérit tout"*— discipline cures everything. Find the right work, these great artists remind us, the work you should be doing, and you will have largely solved the key question of how to spend your life.

This doesn't mean you will be happy all the time. But the work will become an inner citadel to which you can retreat during times of crisis, as well as a reliable rampart from which to face the world and misfortune. As the historian R. H. Tawney once wrote, "If a man has important work to do, and enough leisure and income to enable him to do it properly, he is in possession of as much happiness as is good for any of the children of Adam." Yet almost any work can be important. With an admiration bordering on envy, the contemporary poet Philip Levine used to observe a clothes presser in a Detroit tailor's shop: "I read in his movements not a disregard for this work but, rather, the affirmation that all work was worth doing with elegance and precision and that necessary work granted dignity to the worker. For me he was both a pants presser and the most truly dignified person I'd ever met, one of the unacknowledged legislators of the world."

Levine's words call to mind the classical imperative: "Do what you are doing." That is, whether you are preparing dinner or playing tennis or tuning a car's engine or sweeping a room, really focus your whole self on just that. Do it well, and you can invest even the most trivial activities with significance, transforming the mundane into the spiritual.

A GUIDE FOR THE PERPLEXED

The best book ever written about the relationship between work and leisure remains *Walden*, by Henry David Thoreau. (If you've never read it, read it now.) Its opening chapters and its conclusion, in particular, remind us that what matters in life is to become who we are, and that the only failure is to shrink from this duty and follow instead the dictates of family, society, or religion.

Thoreau writes, "I went to the woods because I wished to live deliberately, to front only the essential facts of life, so that when I came to die I would not discover that I had not lived." That last clause indicates the cost of refusing to acknowledge what one is. Too many people, Thoreau was convinced, allow their lives to be used up in the pursuit of needless wealth and social status; hence his advocacy of simplicity and his advice to keep wants to a minimum. Throughout *Walden* Thoreau persistently asks us to think about a single question: What really matters? Our answer determines how we live, how well we spend those days and nights given to each of us alone. As he reminds us in a famous sentence: "If a man does not keep pace with his companions, perhaps it is because he hears a different drummer. Let him step to that music which he hears, no matter how measured or far away."

DOWNTIME

The ancients believed that leisure was, in the words of the modern philosopher Josef Pieper, "the basis of culture." *Otium*—the Latin for leisure—was essential not only to philosophic inquiry and spiritual receptivity, but also to artistic creativity. Over the centuries writers have regularly written "In Praise of Idleness" (as Robert Louis Stevenson titled one of his best essays). Without periods of downtime, or daydreaming, we find ourselves growing dull, mechanical, enslaved to a routine. We need what Italians call *il dolce far niente*—the pleasure of doing nothing.

Our inner lives are, after all, remarkably wasteful. To come up with a good idea, whether for a building or a poem, a garden or a new hairstyle, requires the mind to explore its options, try out notions, and allow the subconscious to gradually perform its magic. Eventually, there may be a "Eureka" moment, when the scales drop from the eyes and a course of action grows clear. More often, we may simply come up against a deadline and need to start producing.

Nonetheless, during these seemingly fallow periods, which to the world can resemble mere daydreaming, real work is being done. Don't many of us regularly find our best ideas while soaking in the bathtub (like Pythagoras when he cried out that first "Eureka!") or as we drift off to sleep or linger in the pleasant half-awakened lethargy of morning? In these places, at these times, our roiling, restless consciousness is finally quiet, and so schemes and fancies can rise to the surface. Rudyard Kipling believed his own unconscious imagination was guided by his "Daemon," a term taken from the Greek for a personal genius or guardian. Before embarking on a writing project, said Kipling, he sometimes needed to allow his Daemon to perform its secret magic; he needed to "wait, drift and obey."

The function of leisure is essentially to liberate us from too much consciousness. (As Dostoyevsky's Underground Man announced, "Too much consciousness is a disease, a positive disease.") Periodically, we need to break away from the ego's relentless monitoring, forget our packed daily calendars, shake off what the poet Charles Baudelaire described as *"l'horrible fardeau du temps,"*—the horrible burden of time—or what we might now call time pressure. Prayer, meditation, fantasy, intoxication, free association, psychoanalysis, daydreaming, play—all these are techniques for entering a realm of being other than the quotidian, tapping into our inner self, touching something dark and ecstatic in our essence. By doing this regularly, we salve not only our troubled spirits but also our imaginations. "To do good work a man should be industrious," said the preacher Henry Ward Beecher, but "to do great work he must certainly be idle as well."

Much of the time we may be satisfied with quiet philosophic leisure: the even, peaceful tenor of days spent gardening or angling like Izaak Walton or in quiet conversation with friends. Is there a better glimpse of human contentment than the dialogues of Plato or the gently humorous conversation novels—*Crotchet Castle, Gryll Grange*—of Thomas Love Peacock? But sometimes such modest, genteel idleness isn't quite enough.

In C. G. Jung's psychology we only injure our fundamental being by denying the dark and sometimes cruel side of us called the shadow. Nietzsche described the interdependence of the Apollonian (or rational) and the Dionysian (or ecstatic) in ancient Greek civilization. Each of us needs the periodic emotional release of carnival, and so festivals of silliness and excess like Mardi Gras, the Feast of Fools, and the World Turned Upside Down are common to virtually all cultures.

Tension and release, focused work and unfocused relaxation. People, it seems, are locked into binary systems: Too much tension leads to stress, then breakdown, while nothing but idleness makes us soft, lethargic, and swinish. "Why should life all labor be?" sing Tennyson's Lotos-Eaters, before sinking into torpor and lassitude.

The ideal is to embrace our polarities, to choose not a bland, colorless existence, but one where the full spectrum of our personalities, the dark as well as the light, is given its due. Aristotle based his ethics on choosing the mean between two extremes, just as his teacher Plato insisted that a life devoted solely to pleasure would be as incomplete as one given over entirely to wisdom. Only the mixed life is a complete and fulfilled life. Any of us might argue with Plato and even disagree with Aristotle, but it's hard to contend with both.

PLAY'S THE THING

When we consider the ways we might spend our leisure hours—daydreaming, watching sports on TV, surfing the Net, traveling, going to the movies—we shouldn't overlook or neglect hobbies and pets. To build model airplanes, take care of a dog or tank of tropical fish, play serious chess, throw pots, cook new recipes, keep up a scrapbook or a correspondence—all these are active uses of our imagination and yet refresh us because they are seldom the source of our salaries. An amateur, after all, is simply one who loves.

And of all pastimes, those involving us with nature feel especially restorative and right for our souls. The English don Basil Willey movingly wrote: "Solitude, silence, the admonishing presence of grand, fair and permanent forms, and the gentler allurements of pure air, flowers and clear streams—these are amongst the best things we have in this imperfect world; they are valuable in themselves." The bird-watcher who gazes at the majesty of a blue heron skimming along a southern river or the gardener in the early morning weeding among her raised beds of vegetables, the hiker on the Appalachian Trail or the snorkeler in the Caribbean, all these receive the blessing of a mood in which, as Wordsworth said, "the heavy and the weary weight / Of all this unintelligible world, / Is lightened."

Not everyone may respond quite so strongly as Wordsworth to the woods and its wonders, but it behooves each of us to find a similar refuge in our lives, whether it be as a gym rat or an amateur actor, a book collector or a weekend chef. Such activities as these can grant us a peace that passeth understanding.

BLURRING THE BOUNDARIES

Some people try for a clear demarcation between work and leisure. They ride the train to the office or drive to the assembly plant; for eight hours or so, they make phone calls or widgets— and what exactly are widgets?—and then they wearily come home, pull on some jeans, spend the evening in front of the big-screen television or out in the garden, pottering with the heliotropes. After a few hours, they climb the stairs to bed, and the next morning the same process begins again.

Many men and women need the clarity of this austere division: work in this pigeonhole, recreation in that one. But in the world of telecommunications and home offices, it makes sense, when possible, to combine the professional and the personal or, at least, to make easier the transition between the two. To start, one can transform the Danish functional look of traditional business life into something a bit more playful, more reflective of the unique self.

Consider, for example, the place where you actually work.

Freud loaded the top of his desk with figurines, small sculptures, and primitive fetishes, leaving hardly any room for a pencil and pad of paper. Colette kept a collection of snowglobes around her worktable. Even the Marxist playwright Bertolt Brecht liked to have a toy donkey near his writing area, with a bobbing head and a little sign: "I too must understand it." After all, if you're go-

ing to spend hours of your life, day after day, year after year, doing something, why not like where you do it?

Pinned to a bulletin board above where I usually write is an in-
dex card inscribed with a depressing quote from Henry James:
"The practice of 'reviewing' has nothing in common with the art
of criticism." To the right of this card, and perhaps even more
disheartening, is a photocopy of "How to Convert a RoadRunner
Document to Quark-Readable Format." (Such, my friends, is
modern journalism.) Here too is an advertising flyer for a memoir
about dogsledding: *My Lead Dog Was a Lesbian.* Then a photograph of a bombed-out London library. Next to it another scrap
of paper, this one sporting a quotation from Jack Green, an early
champion of the novelist William Gaddis: "Recognizing masterpieces is the job of the critic, not writing competent reviews of the
unimportant."

If I glance at the wall to the right of my monitor, I can study a
1996 calendar from the Lorain Admiral King High School
Marching Band, with a handsome picture of the assembled musicians taken by Fazio's Starlight Studio. Nearby cluster the following:
a photograph of Marilyn Monroe, seated on some playground
equipment, reading James Joyce's *Ulysses;* portraits of several favorite writers, among them Vladimir Nabokov, M. F. K. Fisher,
Jorge Luis Borges, Anton Chekhov, Stendhal; a caricature of
Robertson Davies and a poster of William Joyce's *Dinosaur Bob.*
This last abuts a reproduction of a Roy Lichtenstein painting,
nothing but a pair of staring eyes and these words: "Why did you
say that? What do you know about my image duplicator?" In the
upper-right corner of an adjacent bulletin board looms a picture

of the robot Gort clutching a red-gowned Patricia Neal: an advertisement for *The Day the Earth Stood Still* ("From out of space . . . A warning and an ultimatum!"). Close at hand are several other postcards: the Château d'If near Marseille, where Edmond Dantès was imprisoned before he escaped to become the Count of Monte Cristo; the steel plant in which my father toiled for forty-odd years; Wilder Hall at Oberlin College.

Even the least observant visitor to this "office" could hardly miss the paperback cover that glorifies a stern Conan the Barbarian standing atop a mound of dead enemies while a voluptuous lovely caresses his mighty thigh (I call it "the book critic's dream"); or the button that says "I am a committed radical. I am against nearly everything"; or the color Xerox of the 1926 issue of *Amazing Stories* showing the Martian tripods of H. G. Wells's *War of the Worlds*, or the small poster of Douglas Fairbanks riding a winged horse in *The Thief of Baghdad*, or the photocopy of my late friend Susan Davis's drawing of an owl reading in a library. Also prominent are John Tenniel's illustration of Alice passing through the looking glass, the cover for Martin Rowson's comic-book version of *The Waste Land*, spotlighting a truly sinister T. S. Eliot holding out a handful of dust, and, not least, a bumper sticker that proclaims, "You can afford to be a connoisseur and a rebel" (long my secret wish). I am particularly fond of one other postcard, sent to me by the literary journalist Daphne Merkin, picturing the sorrowful donkey Eeyore bent over a piece of paper with a caption reading: "This writing business, pencils and what-not. Overrated if you ask me."

On my desk itself are—in addition to a phone, Rolodex, and a caddy of pencils and pens—several coffee mugs, a half-dozen pads of paper, no visible work surface whatsoever, and, at this point in time, nearly a dozen books: *The American Heritage Dictionary, The Oxford American Writer's Thesaurus,* a small King James Version of the Bible, a pocket Shakespeare, H. W. Fowler's *Modern English Usage,* the little *Annals of English Literature* (showing the dates of important literary publications from 1475 to 1950), a French dictionary, a German dictionary, an Italian dictionary, and my battered commonplace book into which I copy favorite passages culled from my reading. Pull open my desk drawers, and you will discover more books, as well as reams of correspondence (poorly filed, if at all) and, somewhere, one of those elaborate daily organizers. Periodically, of course, in a token effort toward greater efficiency, I shovel off a few strata of paper, but before long my in-basket again resembles an unemptied wastebasket. Even the cramped space at my feet is crammed with paperbacks, the odd poster, and several more boxes of my all-important papers.

Why, I am sometimes asked, do I burden myself with all this stuff? To visitors I explain, with a wan smile which fools no one, that my work space is a reflection of a singularly capacious and far-ranging intellect, one that observes no boundaries or limits, that boldly goes wherever knowledge is to be had. Pretty feeble.

Of course, I do find the quotes and pictures amusing or heartening; I even refer periodically to the reference books scattered about. But the truth is that my desk is a refuge, a nest, what Cyril Connolly famously called "a womb with a view." Here I am in my element—among books and words and pencils and paper—and so feel secure. In this cozy, cluttered retreat the work will get done.

THE GUEST-ROOM LIBRARY

Say "leisure," and many people will instantly think summer vacation—lying on a beach, snoozing in a hammock under the shade trees, visiting friends in Florida, renting a condo in Cancun. Of course the wise traveler takes his own favorite authors along on holiday, but what if that supply of Georgette Heyer and Dick Francis runs out? In a properly appointed world you would simply borrow from a well-stocked shelf of guest-room books.

Now the essential quality of a proper guest-room book is that it must avoid all the normal requirements of a "good read." Nothing too demanding or white-knuckled suspenseful. Ideally, items should be familiar, cozy, browsable, above all soothing—like the following titles, conveniently arranged according to the major light-reading genres. Each category lists three possible choices. All guest rooms are presumed to start with the Bible, Shakespeare, and at least one novel by Jane Austen.

MYSTERY: 1. Arthur Conan Doyle, *The Complete Sherlock Holmes*. The fog rolls in, the fire burns low, and the game is always afoot. 2. G. K. Chesterton, *The Father Brown Omnibus*. Paradoxes resolved, from an "invisible" man to the hammer of God. 3. Dorothy L. Sayers's anthology, *The Omnibus of Crime*. Brilliant introductory essay on the history of the mystery and supernatural tale, followed by classic examples. (All-American alternative: Dashiell Hammett's *The Maltese Falcon*, Raymond Chandler's *Farewell, My Lovely*, or any Nero Wolfe omnibus by Rex Stout.)

HORROR AND FANTASY: 1. M. R. James, *Collected Ghost Stories.*
Accursed manuscripts, haunted bedclothes, and cozy, antiquarian
chills. 2. John Collier's *Fancies and Goodnights.* Witty Jazz Age
tales of magic elixirs and deals with the devil. 3. *Gods, Men and
Ghosts: The Best Supernatural Fiction of Lord Dunsany* (edited by
E. F. Bleiler). Classic club stories, often told over a large whiskey,
of strange sights, Munchausen-like exploits, and macabre encounters: "The Gibbelins eat, as is well known, nothing less good
than man."

HUMOR: 1. British version: *The Weekend Wodehouse.* Silliness in
the world of spats, aunts, and beautifully crafted sentences. American version: James Thurber, *The Thurber Carnival.* Includes such
classics as "The Night the Bed Fell," "The Macbeth Murder Mystery," and "The Secret Life of Walter Mitty." 2. Flann O'Brien,
The Best of Myles. The funniest man in Ireland, always dreaming
up "services" such as ventriloquist-escorts who carry on both sides
of a sparkling conversation, thus making their companions look
attractive and witty. American alternative: *The Most of S. J. Perelman.* "Diana turned on the radio. With a savage snarl the radio
turned on her . . ." 3. Any of *The New Yorker*'s cartoon books. Or
any album of drawings by Charles Addams, George Price, Peter
Arno, George Booth, Gary Larson, or G. B. Trudeau.

BIOGRAPHY: 1. *The Conversations of Dr. Johnson* (edited by Raymond Postgate). For many, Samuel Boswell's *Life of Johnson* is the
most diverting book in the world; this abridgment highlights the
gruff doctor's grouchy, aphoristic talk. 2. John Aubrey's *Brief*

Lives. Sexual scandals among English worthies of the sixteenth and seventeenth centuries, including Sir Walter Raleigh, who, when he wasn't placing his cloak before the queen, had more than an eye for her maids-in-waiting. 3. Any good collection of letters, such as those of Flannery O'Connor, Gustave Flaubert, or Oliver Wendell Holmes. My own favorite is *The Lyttelton/Hart Davis Letters*, the very literary and gossippy exchanges between a London publisher, Rupert Hart-Davis, and his old Eton teacher, George Lyttelton.

POETRY: 1. W. H. Auden and Norman Holmes Pearson's five-volume *Poets of the English Language*. Dazzling introductions by Auden; a survey of English and American poetry that manages to be both catholic and idiosyncratic. 2. Any of the Oxford books of sixteenth-, seventeenth-, eighteenth-, nineteenth-, or twentieth-century poetry. Some of these, like Philip Larkin's on twentieth-century verse, are surprisingly eccentric and consequently treasure troves of the fine and unfamiliar. 3. The complete works of a favorite poet, such as T. S. Eliot, Alexander Pope, Langston Hughes, Elizabeth Bishop. Sometimes you want to immerse yourself in a single writer's sensibility. However, guest-rooms libraries should probably forgo the later work of Sylvia Plath, Anne Sexton, and John Berryman.

CHILDREN'S CLASSICS: 1. Any good collection of classic fairy tales. Andrew Lang's *Blue Fairy Book* and its successors are semi-standard; these are some of the first, and best, stories we ever hear in our lives. The shortest, most wistful of all? "Once upon a time . . . they lived happily ever after." 2. Lewis Carroll, *Alice in Wonderland* and *Through the Looking-Glass.* "Curiouser and curiouser." More memorable lines per square inch than any other book in English, excepting only Shakespeare's collected plays and the Bible. 3. E. Nesbit, *Five Children and It,* or any of her other classic fantasies for young people. Into the ordinary lives of schoolchildren irrupt adventures and creatures worthy of *The Arabian Nights.*

DEEP—BUT NOT TOO DEEP—THOUGHTS: 1. La Rochefoucauld's *Maxims.* One- or two-sentence observations that you can think about for a moment or for half your life: "The surest way to be outwitted is to suppose yourself sharper than others." "In their first passions women are in love with their lover; in all the rest, with love." 2. Montaigne's *Essays.* In these pages we find a self-portrait of one of the most admirable human beings, and finest writers, of all time. 3. *Seven Greeks,* translated by Guy Davenport. Archilochos, Sappho, Alkman, Anacreon, Heracleitus, Diogenes, Herondas . . . From these founders of Western culture all that tends to remain are tantalizing fragments, and they are just right for late-night meditations. "A bow is alive only when it kills" is one example, by Heracleitus.

REFERENCE: 1. Any of the *Oxford Companion* volumes—to English, French, or classical literature; any of the Oxford books of political anecdotes, marriage, death, or dreams; Brewer's *Dictionary of Phrase and Fable;* any odd volumes of the *Dictionary of National Biography.* All of these are standbys of bedside browsing.

2. H. W. Fowler's *Modern English Usage*. Not only a guide to grammar, Fowler offers quirky, addictive mini-essays on every aspect of language. 3. *The New Columbia Encyclopedia*. One volume containing nearly all knowledge. Ideal for serendipitous reading or finding out the difference between a quark and a quasar.

JOURNALS AND DIARIES. 1. *The Diary of Virginia Woolf*, five volumes. Gossip becomes literature. 2. *Pages from the Goncourt Journal* (chosen and translated by Robert Baldick). Gossip about women, art, society, and illness, starring Gustave Flaubert, Emile Zola, Guy de Maupassant, and other high-living French authors. 3. *The Diary of Samuel Pepys*. Observant, funny, and touching. "And so to bed."

ODDS AND ENDS: Any guest room should always include some personal favorites, though it is prudent to provide only "borrowable" copies. Edward Gorey's little albums of the macabre. E. V. Lucas and George Morrow's *What a Life!*—that improbable Edwardian-Surrealist classic. Martin Gardner's various collections of mathematical games and speculations. Cyril Connolly's moody, aphoristic "word cycle," *The Unquiet Grave*. Robert Phelps and Peter Deane's scrapbook-almanac, *The Literary Life*. E. F. Bleiler's definitive *Guide to Supernatural Fiction*, which summarizes the plots of some strange, strange tales. The endlessly browsable *Encyclopedia of Science Fiction* and *Encyclopedia of Fantasy*, by John Clute and John Grant and others.

And, oh yes, one last item: the latest edition of Leonard Maltin's annual guide to movies—just in case.

Four

THE BOOKS OF LOVE

Love is holy because it is like grace—the worthiness of its object is
never really what matters.   — MARILYNNE ROBINSON

EROS IS EROS IS EROS

"I had fallen so low," writes the young Englishman in Nikos
Kazantzakis' novel *Zorba the Greek*, "that if I had had to choose
between falling in love with a woman and reading a book about
love, I should have chosen the book." This sounds pitiful—
happily, the young scholar soon changes his ways—and yet love and
writing seem always to have gone together, hand in hand. Even
now, the starry-eyed frequently find themselves composing sonnets and buying little volumes of Sappho and Rumi. Our earliest

Greek poet, Archilochos, sighed like any adolescent, "If only it were my fortune just to touch Neoboule's hand."

At the same time books have caused lovers no end of trouble. Paolo and Francesca, bound together in Dante's Hell, fell into adultery over the story of the illicit affair between Sir Lancelot and Guinevere: "That day we read no further." Emma Bovary, in Flaubert's novel, might never have strayed from her dull husband were it not for those dreamy romances she devoured when young. And has any man ever lived up to the ideal of Jane Austen's Darcy or Emily Bronte's Heathcliff?

THE COURSE OF LOVE (PART ONE)

Imagine a yearlong seminar on everyone's favorite emotion. Which poems, stories, and plays should be on the syllabus? And why? Here, in roughly chronological order, are some of the masterworks in the literature of love.

Sappho, poetic fragments. The great celebrant of "Eros, the bittersweet."
Eros make me shiver again
Strengthless in the knees,
Eros gall and honey,
Snake-sly, invincible.
—Sappho (translated by Guy Davenport)

Plato, *The Symposium*. In this most beautiful of Plato's dialogues, a group of friends drinks the night away as they discuss the nature of love. Two ideas about Eros, often much simplified, have proved especially influential: Aristophanes claims that human beings were once round ball-like creatures that the gods divided in two. Each of us is in restless search of his or her missing half. In his turn, Socrates tells us that he learned from a wise woman named Diotima about a "ladder of love." We typically begin by desiring the physically beautiful, but we should then ascend through stages of increasing spirituality to a contemplation of the transcendentally beautiful, good, and true. Such is the origin of the concept of "platonic love."

Catullus, Horace, Ovid—selected poems. Three classic celebrants of physical desire, jealousy, and suffering. Catullus famously pleads with his beloved for "a thousand kisses, then a hundred, another thousand next, another hundred." The moderate epicurean Horace reminds us that life is short and we must live for the moment, "*carpe diem*"—seize the day. Ovid's *Amores* chronicles jealousy and sadism; his *Ars Amatoria* discusses love's "techniques," from flirtation to quite explicit sexual positions.

Courtly love. Inspired by Arabic poetry, the cult of the Virgin Mary, and the necessary feudal obeisance to the lady of a castle when her lord was away on crusade, courtly love softened and feminized men's sexual conduct. As most of this *amour courtois* was adulterous—a marriage being primarily a business arrangement between families—the aspirant to a lady's favor had to prove his worthiness. He must be a "parfit, gentil knyght" (Chaucer's phrase) or demonstrate an unwavering devotion. One troubadour poet worshiped a woman he had never seen, only heard about. Andreas Castellanus even formulated the exacting rules of "the art of courtly love"; for example, the properly infatuated should always turn pale in the presence of his lady.

The classic introduction to twelfth-century Provencal poetry—the heart of the courtly love tradition—is Ezra Pound's enthusiastic (if sometimes historically inaccurate) *The Spirit of Romance*. The most provocative analysis, and critique, of the courtly love tradition remains Denis De Rougemont's influential *Love in the Western World*. "Happy love," laments De Rougemont, "has no history—in European literature. . . . Unless the course of love is being hindered there is no romance; and it is romance that we revel in—that is to say, the self-consciousness, intensity, variations, and delays of passion."

The tales of King Arthur. The Arthurian cycle describes nearly every sort of love, from raw desire to spiritual transcendence. Indeed, the story of Tristan and Isolde manages to blend them, an alchemy best experienced in the glorious music of Wagner's opera. (Mothers in the late nineteenth century refused to allow their daughters to listen to Isolde's ecstatic *Liebestod*, or love-death; there was no mistaking what those crescendos were emulating.) The student of literary love should read at least parts of Thomas Malory's saga of the "once and future king," *Le Morte D'Arthur*. The fullest account of Tristan is that by Gottfried von

Strassburg, while for Perceval and his quest for the Holy Grail one needs to turn to the *Parzival* of Wolfram von Eschenbach, the supreme masterpiece of Middle High German literature. Still, for a single sampling of courtly love, the best choice is probably Chrétien de Troyes's *Lancelot: Or, The Knight of the Cart.*

In this verse-romance, Chrétien de Troyes relates how Queen Guinevere is spirited away to the mysterious land of Gorre, and Sir Lancelot naturally gallops off to her rescue. Early on he loses his horse but happens upon a dwarf with a cart, really a tumbril intended to convey criminals to the gallows. The dwarf tells the knight that if he wants to see Guinevere again he should climb onto the cart. Lancelot hesitates for a moment, then does so, even though he feels deeply ashamed to be viewed by the mocking populace in such a disgraceful vehicle. Eventually, after crossing a sword bridge and enduring much suffering, Lancelot reaches Guinevere, who treats him with cold disdain. The poor fellow is mystified. By this point, he's undergone ordeal after ordeal for this woman. Could any lover have shown himself more faithful? Finally, Guinevere explains. She had been locked in a high tower and could observe Lancelot when he encountered the dwarf. So? Didn't he get into the cart of shame? Yes, Guinevere tells him, but anyone who claimed to love her would not have hesitated for even a moment. It is a long time before Lancelot is restored to the queen's good graces.

Love in the Renaissance. The spiritualization of woman reaches its zenith in Dante's adoration of Beatrice, first in his *Vita Nuova* ("The New Life"), later in *The Divine Comedy*, and then in

Petrarch's influential poems about Laura. In both cases, the poets worshiped their (married) lady from afar until she died young, and then they sang her praises in their poetry. Petrarch, in particular, inaugurated a European craze for sonnet sequences addressed to idealized women.

Still, by the sixteenth century the depiction of love was gradually growing less improbably spiritual and more human. Shakespeare's sonnets chronicle a complex entanglement, almost a ménage à trois, among two men and a woman. In France the essayist Montaigne was once asked why he so loved his deceased friend Etienne de la Béotie. His answer is probably the most sensible ever given to this perennial question: "If you pressed me to say why I loved him, I can say no more than it was because he was he and I was I."

And then in the songs and sonnets of John Donne we finally hear a voice that sounds as urgent and real as our own. "For God's sake, hold your tongue and let me love!" Donne can be delightedly bawdy in the notorious poem commonly called "On His Mistress Going to Bed": "Licence my roving hands, and let them go, / Before, behind, between, above, below. / O my America, my new-found-land!" Or amorously philosophical, as in "The Extasie": "Love's mysteries in soule's doe grow, / But yet the body is his booke." The unexpurgated carpe diem theme would be fully exploited by the seventeenth-century Cavalier poets, especially the earl of Rochester and Sir John Suckling, though its most famous touchstone is certainly Andrew Marvell's "To His Coy Mistress." Every line has passed into the vocabulary of seduction, from the opening "Had we but world enough and time" to the famous summarizing couplet, midway through the poem: "The grave's a fine and private place / But none I think do there embrace."

Such blunt truths about life and sex would find their most expert analyst in the French aristocrat, La Rochefoucauld, who gazed unflinchingly at the behavior of men and women, then recorded what he saw in steely maxims. "There are few good women who do not tire of their role." "There are successful marriages, but no blissful ones." "What keeps lovers and mistresses from tiring of being together is that they talk of nothing but themselves."

A STREETCAR NAMED DESIRE

Make me chaste . . . but not just yet.—Saint Augustine

Twinned helplessness / Against the huge tug of procreation.
—Robert Graves

The principal sin . . . with which the tongue is particularly connected is lust, for, since the days of Eve and the serpent . . . seduction lies in talk, and the tongue is seduction's tool.—Marina Warner

She was only a singularly handsome girl, looking up at him with a shy questioning yet almost trustful air. His good resolutions suddenly broke down. Soon the world and its inhabitants seemed nothing to him, nor would he have stretched out a hand to save them from instant destruction.—Murasaki Shikubu

. . . The rites
In which love's beauteous empress most delights,
Are banquets, Doric music, midnight revel,
Plays, masques, and all that stern age counteth evil.
—Christopher Marlowe

The hind that would be mated to the lion / Must die for love.
—William Shakespeare

The pleasure of love lies in loving, and our own sensations make
us happier than those we inspire.—La Rochefoucauld

Nothing sharpens the wits like promiscuous flirtation.
—George Moore

I don't think I shall ever meet with so delicious an armful again.
—Robert Burns

            We sit and talk,
quietly, with long lapses of silence
and I am aware of the stream
that has no language, coursing
beneath the quiet heaven of
your eyes
            which has no speech; to
go to bed with you, to pass beyond
the moment of meeting, while the
currents float still in mid-air, to

fall—
with you from the brink, before
the crash—

       to seize the moment.
—William Carlos Williams

I love being in love with you. It makes even unhappiness seem no bigger than a pin, even at the times when I wish so violently that I could give my heart to science and be rid of it.—James Schuyler

Humphrey Bogart was "so contemptuous of other men's needs to publicize their amorous triumphs that he refused to notice them. Being supremely confident of his own attractiveness to women, he scorned every form of demonstrativeness. When a woman appealed to him, he waited for her the way the flame waits for the moth."—Louise Brooks

The immediate tactility, the electric curiosity that bodies have for each other: that is real. It is a fuel that keeps one benign and going, something to make the world expand no matter that one day the same world will abruptly contract to measure six feet by two. To say Again in a kerosene-scented room in Egypt is, at that moment, to have made no bad choices and not to have failed.
—James Hamilton-Paterson

I thought you would most likely be rather amused, rather touched, by my importunity. I thought you would take a listless advantage,

make a plaything of me—the diversion of a few idle hours in summer, and then, when you had tired of me, would cast me aside, forget me, break my heart. I desired nothing better than that. That is what I must have been vaguely hoping for.
—Max Beerbohm (from *Zuleika Dobson*).

. . . and how he kissed me under the Moorish wall and I thought well as well him as another and then I asked him with my eyes to ask again yes and then he asked me would I yes to say yes my mountain flower and first I put my arms around him yes and drew him down to me so he could feel my breasts all perfume yes and his heart was going like mad and yes I said yes I will Yes.
—James Joyce (the closing lines of *Ulysses*)

The poet Ezra Pound, interred at St. Elizabeths Hospital for the insane, once told the critic Hugh Kenner, "Sometimes the guards come to me, for a piece of verse to give their sweethearts." "And do you write it?" asked Kenner. "Oh, yes," answered Pound.
—Ezra Pound to Hugh Kenner

THE COURSE OF LOVE (PART TWO)

Stendhal, *On Love*. In *De l'amour* the novelist Stendhal tabulates the psychological impulses behind every aspect of Eros (not excluding unexpected "failure" or impotence). The most celebrated chapters analyze what happens when we fall in love. A bare branch, Stendhal tells us, may be left in the depths of a salt mine, and after a few months it will be covered with "shimmering, glittering diamonds, so that the original bough is no longer recognizable." A similar "crystallization," he says, forms around an adored mistress, to whom our minds attribute every beauty and perfection. A young woman may appear quite ordinary to the world's eyes, but to the man in her thrall even her little tics and whimsies are suddenly bathed in a celestial light.

In Steven Millhauser's "An Adventure of Don Juan" (from *The King in the Tree: Three Novellas*), Don Juan—much to his surprise—actually falls in love with a young Englishwoman named Georgiana. "At night, lying restlessly awake, he posed questions to himself that seemed crucial and unanswerable. . . . If you were allowed one night of bliss in the arms of Georgiana, followed immediately by banishment, or a lifetime of chaste friendship, which would you choose? If you were permitted to ravish Georgiana night after night for the next ten years with the knowledge that she despised you, or to leave tomorrow with the knowledge that she loved you passionately, which would you choose?" Millhauser superbly evokes the agonies of desire—"continual agitation and anxious brooding modified by moments of uncertain hope." Finally, one night Don Juan vows to act. "For love," he tells himself, "is not a sad man sitting under a tree, but a raging sword flashing with blood and fire."

The major novels. Courtship and illicit passion are the two principal themes of modern fiction. Many of the most famous English novels end with a marriage—*Tom Jones, Pride and Prejudice, Jane Eyre*—but most of the great European masterpieces close on heartbreak and death. Women dominate the nineteenth century's obsession with adultery, most famously in Leo Tolstoy's *Anna Karenina* and Theodor Fontane's *Effi Briest* (see below for *Madame Bovary*). By the turn of the century, even English-speaking novelists give us their tragic heroines, like Edith Wharton's Lily Bart in *The House of Mirth* and Thomas Hardy's Tess in *Tess of the D'Urbervilles*.

In the first half of the twentieth century, though, the focus shifts more to men lost to impossible or even unlawful desires, or to unbearable jealousy: Machado de Assis's bitter *Dom Casmurro*, Proust's *In Search of Lost Time* (especially the almost stand-alone novella of obsession, "Swann in Love"), F. Scott Fitzgerald's *The Great Gatsby*, Thomas Mann's *Death in Venice*, Ford Madox Ford's *The Good Soldier* ("This is the saddest story I have ever heard"), and Vladimir Nabokov's *Lolita* ("Light of my life, fire of my loins"). Yearning is what connects nearly all these books, the longing for an elusive, usually unattainable happiness.

Gustave Flaubert, *Madame Bovary.* Not only one of the summits of prose art, but also the most sustained and intense look at a woman's restless search for love in modern fiction. In *Madame Bovary* Flaubert can suggest years of boredom in a paragraph, capture a character in a short conversational exchange, or show us the gulf between his soulful heroine, Emma Bovary, and her complacent husband, Charles, in a single sentence (one that, moreover, presages all Emma's later experience of men). Returning from their wedding, the couple and the bridal party must cross a farmer's field: "Emma's dress was rather long and the hem trailed a bit;

from time to time she would stop and lift it up, then, with gloved fingers, delicately remove the wild grasses and tiny thistle burrs, while Charles stood empty-handed, waiting for her to finish." (Margaret Mauldon's translation) Flaubert may have intended us to regard his heroine as essentially shallow, even kitsch, a creature formed by impossible reveries of blissful self-fulfillment— whether in marriage, passion, or religious observance. Yet it's hard not to sympathize with the doomed young woman. For Emma tries, and tries hard, to live her dreams and in this sense is hardly different from, say, Fitzgerald's Gatsby. Or any of the rest of us. Don't we all ache with unabashed hopes, unassuageable desires? As time passes, Madame Bovary recalls a ball at La Vaubyessard as the single golden interlude in her drab life, a glimpse of paradise. Even so, "little by little, in her memory, the faces all blurred together; she forgot the tunes of the quadrilles; no longer could she so clearly picture the liveries and the rooms; some details disappeared, but the yearning remained." The yearning always remains.

For the modern reader, familiar with adultery, through magazine articles, television soap operas, and (possibly) personal experience, *Madame Bovary* shows how astonishingly common, even standardized is the blueprint for such illicit affairs: the soft-focused imaginings, the touch of a hand, a suggestive phrase or smile, the search for seclusion, the breathless rush to the lover's arms, the fear of exposure, the financial outlay (and the need to hide it), the ever-growing recklessness, and then, more and more often, the violent arguments and impossible demands, the violation of promises, mutual recrimination, and finally, inevitably, the tearful breakup, leading to further heartache, embitterment, and, sometimes, relief. As Flaubert writes about the last days of Emma's affair with Léon, "They knew one another too well to experience that wonderment of mutual possession that increases its joy a hundredfold. She was as sick of him as he was weary of her. Emma was discovering, in adultery, all the banality of marriage."

Some early critics complained that Emma's story was a sordid and common one; yet that is, paradoxically, its glory. Her creator famously proclaimed that he himself was Madame Bovary—but failed to add that so are you, so am I. We are all the victims of unrealizable dreams, which shimmer so alluringly before our eyes, but just a little beyond our reach. "I admire tinsel as much as gold," Flaubert once wrote in a letter. "Indeed, the poetry of tinsel is even greater, because it is sadder."

And what of poetry itself? Virtually every poet writes about love, sooner or later, and some write about almost nothing else. In English one can read Byron's witty narrative poem *Don Juan* ("And sighing 'I will ne'er consent,' consented") or George Meredith's heartbreaking account of a marriage coming apart, *Modern Love* ("Then each applied to each that fatal knife, / Deep questioning, which probes to endless dole"). Tennyson rhapsodizes of youth longing for kisses "sweet as those by hopeless fancy feigned / On lips that are for others," while Swinburne decadently celebrates "Our Lady of Pain" and "the raptures and roses of vice." At the beginning of the nineteenth century Keats proclaims, "Forever wilt thou love, and she be fair!" and at its end Ernest Dowson blithely confides, "I have been faithful to thee, Cynara, in my fashion."

Perhaps the best approach to the poetry of love is through an anthology like Walter de la Mare's *Love*. De la Mare, a poet, novelist, and short-story writer, was also an editor of genius. In *Love* he offers a 135-page introductory essay, followed by 700 pages of prose extracts and poems. The result is admittedly old-fashioned, including plenty of minor Georgian and keepsake verse, yet it is so packed a book, it seems inexhaustible. Open it at random, and you will find, for instance, Dante Gabriel Rossetti's translation of a celebrated François Villon ballad:

Tell me now in what hidden way is
Lady Flora, the lovely Roman?
Where's Hipparchia, and where is Thais,
Neither of them the fairer woman?
Where is Echo, beheld of no man,
Only heard on river and mere,—
She whose beauty was more than human? . . .
But where are the snows of yesteryear?

Turn another page, and there is an even more famous ballad:

In Dublin's fair city, where the girls are so pretty,
I first set my eyes on sweet Mollie Malone,
As she wheeled her wheel-barrow through streets broad and
    narrow
Crying, "Cockles and mussels: alive, alive O!"

. . .

Love in our time. To write a good modern novel about love one must balance art against the pull of sentimentality and the temptations of sexual description. Too much of one or the other, and you end up with either a shopgirl romance or a marital aid. But among the novels of the last quarter of the twentieth century, these ten achieve near perfection in their very different visions of "Eros the bittersweet."

1. James Salter, *Light Years*. A beautifully composed story of a perfect marriage (and family) slowly breaking down, its sentences like drops of rainwater: "Life is weather. Life is meals. Lunches on a blue-checked cloth on which salt has spilled. The smell of tobacco. Brie, yellow apples, wood-handled knives."

2. Alexander Theroux, *Darconville's Cat*. "Darconville, the schoolmaster, always wore black." This impassioned, original novel chronicles obsession, jealousy, and hate with a learned diction (and humor) as magnificent as any in the 17th century. For even more than Darconville loves the college student Isabel, Alexander Theroux loves the heavenly labials and ranting gutturals of the English language. At one moment he can use a word like "deipnosophist" (a person skilled in the art of dining and table talk) and in the next write with utter simplicity: "September: it was the most beautiful of words, he'd always felt, evoking orange-flowers, swallows, and regret."

3. John Crowley, *Little, Big*. The most admired postwar American fantasy, this wistful love story begins when a young man marries a very special young woman. The Drinkwater clan resides in a turn-of-the-century house that seems to grow bigger the farther you go into it; their family photo album includes pictures of elves; and they turn out to be major players in the secret history of the world. The diminuendo of the book's closing sentences evokes its sad autumnal magic: "The world is older than it was. Even the weather isn't as we remember it clearly once being, never lately does there come a summer day such as we remember, never clouds as white as that, never grass as odorous or shade as deep and full of promise as we remember they can be, as once upon a time they were."

4. A. S. Byatt, *Possession: A Romance*. Two modern scholars search for the truth about a secret love affair between two eminent Victorian poets, the consequences of which spread out far more widely than suspected, even into the present. "I read your mind, my dear Mr. Ash. You will argue now for a monitored and carefully limited combustion . . . and there will be—Conflagration."

5. Arundhati Roy, *The God of Small Things*. "They all crossed into forbidden territory. They all tampered with laws that lay down who should be loved and how. And how much." This Booker Prize winner chronicles the heartbreaking story of a doomed affair between a young Indian woman and an untouchable, as well as its effect on two young children, Estha and Rahel. Arundhati Roy

structures her novel so that it builds to a final chapter of incandescent sexual ecstasy, even as we know too well the horror that will follow. Much of the beauty of the book arises from its similes: "It was raining when Rahel came back to Ayemenem. Slanting silver ropes slammed into the loose earth, plowing it up like gunfire."

6. Penelope Fitzgerald, *The Blue Flower*. There is no waste in this apparently meandering, almost leisurely short novel. Written when its author was approaching eighty, it revolves around the love of the German romantic poet Novalis for an insignificant and rather plain young girl of fifteen. In merely 200 pages, Fitzgerald evokes a vanished world, the follies and realities of love, yearning and suffering. Even its minor characters are indelible. A successful surgeon realizes that the woman with whom he grew infatuated when young has forgotten his name: "What means something to us, that we can name. Sink, he told his hopes, with a kind of satisfaction, sink like a corpse dropped into the river. I am rejected, not for being unwelcome, not even for being ridiculous, but for being nothing."

7. Ferdinand Mount, *Fairness*. "How cool and objective we mean to sound, how hot our hearts." In this funny and heartbreaking novel, a rather staid Englishman finds his life ruined by a woman he adores and can never possess. "She ties men up in knots," a character warns him, "just because her hair looks like a bunch of hay. If her follicles had a different juice in them, you wouldn't think twice about her."

8. Edmund White, *The Married Man*. You might read this novel while listening to the slow jazz of a weary-hearted sax player. *The Married Man* is a winning portrait of gay Paris in the 1980s, a satire of American university life, a semi-autobiographical portrait of the artist, an unsparing AIDS chronicle, but above all it is an utterly convincing love story. White's plangent, autumnal voice—like a loved one's whisper in the night—gradually summons up a lost world of wit and languor, of champagne dinners and simple lunches on sun-dappled terraces. But gradually this earthly paradise gives way to T-cell counts, and the novel's last quarter is a journey into the dark.

9. Philip Roth, *The Dying Animal*. A harrowing short novel about a cultivated man of seventy, a lifelong hedonist, who takes up with a voluptuous twenty-four-year-old student. After a period of the sheerest lust, Roth's hero suddenly finds himself suffering "these crazy distortions of longing, doting, possessiveness, even of love." Without quite knowing it, he confesses, "attachment creeps in. The eternal problem of attachment."

10. Zadie Smith, *On Beauty*. "People talk about the happy quiet that can exist between two lovers, but this too was great; sitting between his sister and his brother, saying nothing, eating. . . ." This masterly novel takes up the myriad forms of Eros—first love, family happiness, irrational and illicit desire—and does so in language that can mirror the cultured speech of a British academic or the hip-hop patter of a black street poet. In the end, the reader

falls in love with the entire Belsey family, in all its quarrelsome, well-meaning confusion.

THE WISDOM OF EXPERIENCE

The magic of first love is our ignorance that it can ever end.
—Benjamin Disraeli

The reason why so few marriages are happy is because young ladies spend their time in making nets, not in making cages.
—Jonathan Swift

Much can be inferred about a man from his mistress: in her one beholds his weaknesses and his dreams.—Georg Lichtenberg

Were it not for imagination, Sir, a man would be as happy in the arms of a chambermaid as of a Duchess.—Samuel Johnson

Such things as an absence, the refusal of an invitation, or an unintentional coldness accomplish more than all the cosmetics and fine clothes in the world.—Marcel Proust

No man is offended by another man's admiration of the woman he loves; it is the woman only who can make it a torment.
—Jane Austen

To fall in love is to create a religion that has a fallible god.
—Jorge Luis Borges

Romanticism is what brings a couple together, but realism is what sees them through.—John Updike

The truth is that what is interesting about love is how it doesn't work out.—Howard Moss

That which we call sin in others, is experiment for us.
—Ralph Waldo Emerson

Man survives earthquakes, epidemics, the horror of disease, and all the agonies of the soul, but for all time his most tormenting tragedy has been, is, and will be the tragedy of the bedroom.—Leo Tolstoy

The best of men and the best of women may sometimes live together all their lives, and . . . hold each other lost spirits to the end.—Robert Louis Stevenson

It is never any good dwelling on good-bys. It is not the being together that it prolongs, it is the parting.—Elizabeth Bibesco

For a dark play-girl in a night-club I have pined away. . . . If this thoughtless woman were to die there would be nothing left to live for, if this faithless girl forgot me there would be no one for whom to write.—Cyril Connolly

After discovering that his wife had left him for another man: "I did not know it was possible to be so miserable and live but I am told that this is a common experience."—Evelyn Waugh

She wasn't too big, heroic, what they call Junoesque. It was that there was just too much of what she was for any one human female package to contain, and hold: too much of white, too much of female, too much of maybe just glory, I don't know: so that at first sight of her you felt a kind of shock of gratitude just for being alive and being male at the same instant with her in space and time, and then in the next second and forever after a kind of despair because you knew that there never would be enough of any one male to match and hold and deserve her; grief forever after because forever after nothing less would ever do.—William Faulkner

We were never to be alone together again, except in remembrance. —Walter de la Mare

I'm ninety-four years . . . and my mind is just a turmoil of regrets. . . . In the summer of 1902 I came real close to getting in serious trouble with a married woman, but I had a fight with my conscience and my conscience won, and what's the result? I had two wives, good, Christian women, and I can't hardly remember what either of them looked like, but I can remember the face of that woman so clear it hurts, and there's never a day passes I don't think about her, and there's never a day passes I don't curse myself. "What kind of a timid, dried up, weevily fellow were you?" I say to myself. "You should've said to hell with what's right and what's wrong, the devil take the hindmost. You'd have something to remember, you'd be happier now." She's out in Woodlawn, six feet under, and she's been there twenty-two years, God rest her, and here I am, just an old, old man with nothing left but a belly and a brain and a dollar or two.—Joseph Mitchell

Occasionally in the middle of a conversation her name would be mentioned, and she would run down the steps of a chance sentence, without turning her head.—Vladimir Nabokov

The only victory over love is flight.—Napoleon Bonaparte

TETE-A-TETE

The novelist Arnold Bennett once estimated that "not in one per cent, even of romantic marriages are the husband and wife capable of *passion* for each other after three years. So brief is the violence of love! In perhaps thirty-three per cent passion settles down into a tranquil affection—which is ideal. In fifty percent it sinks into sheer indifference, and one becomes used to one's wife or husband as to one's other habits. And in the remaining sixteen per cent it develops into dislike or detestation."

This is bitter wisdom indeed, and yet it conforms to what science now tells us about hormones, endorphins, and the short-lived phenomenon called limerance. Sexual infatuation requires separation, obstacles, distance. One cannot dwell in a white heat for long.

But a fortunate marriage offers more than mere "tranquil affection." It is, in essence, a civilization of two, and its greatest joy

is a conversation that goes on for decades. Such intercourse between husband and wife, or between committed partners of any
sex, requires time to develop and is, along with children, the real
foundation for domestic happiness. Yet there is, wrote the novelist
Robertson Davies in a letter, "a persistent idea that a marriage
must be the continuation of a romance, when a minute's reflection
shows that it can be nothing of the kind. It must be an association
of people of similar or complementary tastes who enter it with a
firm resolve to make it work."

Shared memories, common pursuits, reliable support during
times of crisis, even the same old arguments—these matter more
than young people commonly realize. As the actress Mrs. Patrick
Campbell once wrote: after the hurly-burly of the chaise longue
comes the deep, deep peace of the double bed.

BRINGING IT ALL BACK HOME

What the mother sings to the cradle goes all the way down to the
coffin.`
—HENRY WARD BEECHER

WE ARE WHAT WE READ

Dr. Seuss (Theodore Geisel) has written more immortal works
than any other twentieth-century American author. Think about
it: Virtually every child in this country has read, is reading, or will
read *The Cat in the Hat, Horton Hears a Who, And to Think that I
Saw It on Mulberry Street, The Butter Battle Book,* and perhaps a
dozen others equally splendid. Consider too that each of Seuss's
more than forty titles is read not once, not twice, but scores of
times, usually to pieces. In a library they become, literally, things
of shreds and patches.

And what do we learn from Seuss? The joy of words and pictures at play, of course, but also the best and most humane values any of us might wish to possess: pluck, determination, tolerance, reverence for the earth, suspicion of the martial spirit, the fundamental value of the imagination.

This is why early reading matters. At any age, but especially in childhood, books can transform lives. As Graham Greene once wrote, "In childhood all books are books of divination, telling us about the future, and like the fortune teller who sees a long journey in the cards or death by water they influence the future." For the young are all what college English professors would label "bad" readers: They identify with a story's hero or heroine, and they daydream about being as resourceful as the Boxcar Children, as brave as Brave Irene, as clever as Dido Twite or Ulysses. And what children behold, they become.

ONCE UPON A TIME

As a boy I never read *Winnie-the-Pooh* or *The Wind in the Willows*, *Peter Pan* or *Charlotte's Web*. Perhaps our local library didn't stock them, or maybe I judged such works too feminine for the tough guy buried inside my pudgy, nearsighted body. Once I could actually read, and my mother turned her pedagogical attentions to my younger sisters, my dad started to take me regularly to the Lorain Public Library. There I checked out *Curious George*, *The Five Chinese Brothers*, and Danny Dunn's series of misadventures with antigravity paint and homework machines. I vividly recall *Miss*

Pickerell Goes to Mars and *Treasure at First Base* and the maritime derring-do of Howard Pease's young heroes. A little later my elementary school class joined a paperback book club, and I soon began to build my own personal library: *Big Red, Secret Sea, Mystery of the Piper's Ghost, Snow Treasure, Revolt on Alpha C, Mystery of the Spanish Cave.*

In fifth grade the book club's newsletter offered three of the best adventure stories ever written: Jules Verne's *Journey to the Center of the Earth,* Arthur Conan Doyle's *The Lost World* and *The Hound of the Baskervilles.* What has ever been better than to be ten years old with books like these to open on dark and stormy evenings? Late one happy fall I settled down with the complete adventures of Sherlock Holmes and Father Brown, as well as Verne's *The Mysterious Island,* all checked out from the branch library in the kind of thick volumes you could live in for weeks.

Alas, city libraries then refused to stock many popular juvenile potboilers, in particular the innumerable exploits of the Hardy Boys and Tarzan; still, one could always unearth yet one more new adventure of these and other similarly resilient heroes in the cluttered basements of neighbors and relatives. To this day, I remember a certain Saturday afternoon, a paper bag of candy corn, and the sun streaming onto the glorious pages of *Tom Swift in the Caves of Nuclear Fire.* Life has been downhill ever since.

By the time I finished elementary school my tastes had shifted to grown-up novels of the fast-moving sort: Sax Rohmer's Fu Manchu thrillers, the science fiction of Robert Heinlein, the adventures of James Bond. For many years thereafter I utterly disdained "kiddie lit." In my midthirties, though, I unexpectedly found myself asked to add children's literature to my responsibilities as a writer and editor for *Book World*. Being conscientious, I consulted librarians about recommended reading, checked out several dozen juvenile classics, and studied the criticism and history of the field. Somewhat to my surprise, I found myself particularly entranced by the complex synergy of words and illustrations in classic picture books.

As I would learn, the late 1970s and '80s ushered in another golden age of children's literature to rival the earlier one of *Peter Rabbit* and *The Wizard of Oz*. Think of just a few of the authors, artists and eye-popping works of that era: Maurice Sendak's complex *Outside over There*, numerous masterpieces by Chris Van Allsburg, including *Jumanji* and *The Mysteries of Harris Burdick*, William Joyce's *Dinosaur Bob* and *A Day with Wilbur Robinson*, picture books by Leo and Diane Dillon, William Steig's *Dr. De Soto* and *Shrek*, David McCullough's *Black and White*, Jon Scieszka and Lane Smith's *The True Story of the Three Little Pigs*, and those are just the beginning. The past thirty or so years have also seen Gary Paulsen's survivalist adventure *Hatchet*, Phyllis Reynolds Naylor's classic *Shiloh*, award-winning novels by Katherine Paterson and Walter Dean Myers, Russell Hoban's touching fable *The Marzipan Pig*, the metaphysical comedies of Daniel Pinkwater, Joan Aiken's rambunctious tales of Dido Twite, and the intricate fantasies of Alan Garner, Richard Kennedy, and Diana Wynne Jones. And let's not overlook that most elegantly structured of all juvenile time-travel novels, the gravely beautiful *Tom's Midnight Garden* by Philippa Pearce.

Then came the tsunami of J. K. Rowling's Harry Potter books, shortly followed by—in my view—the finer but more controversial fantasies of Philip Pullman (*The Golden Compass, The Subtle Knife, The Amber Spyglass*). More and more adults began to read "kiddie" books—and not aloud to their offspring but on the beach, in bed, and at the beauty parlor.

Obviously I should have been one happy children's book reviewer, but another development of the 1980s troubled me. In 1950s Ohio, a boy could slide easily into daydreams about King Solomon's mines, mysterious islands, swordplay in Ruritania, cackling master criminals, and dark avengers. Books fed the imagination. Then suddenly CD-ROMs, video games, and digitalized movies began to surpass any child's wildest fantasies. But all they exercised, as far as I could tell, was hand-eye coordination. Yet more and more it grew clear that computer monitors and widescreen TVs were becoming, in Keats's phrase, "charmed magic casements" to transport us to "faery lands forlorn."

While I sometimes think it's wrong to be concerned, it *has* been a long while since I glimpsed a kid sprawled under a shade tree lost in a book. After all, we can't count on J. K. Rowling alone to create or sustain a passion for turning pages. Like Aristotelian virtue, reading is a habit. Children need to read, then to read some more. Quantity matters far more than quality—there will be plenty of time for classics. But when starting out, the young should be immersed in a culture of the sentence, not the screen.

THE CHILDREN'S HOUR

Anxious parents—are there any other kind?—long for advice on just how they can encourage their kids to read more. Here are some suggestions, most of which fall into the category of common sense.

1. Read aloud to your children. Joan Aiken once said, "If you're not prepared to read to your children an hour a day, you shouldn't have any."

2. Read yourself. Grown-ups often pay lip service to the joys of reading, but do the kids see you watching TV or do they see you with a book in your hands? Here is the litmus test: How often have you said to your child, "Just a minute, I want to finish this chapter"?

3. Fill your house with print. There should be paperbacks, comics, magazines, and newspapers everywhere the children look. Books should be a part of a family's daily life, not something special. Ideally, each member of the household should have his or her own bookcase.

4. Visit the library and bookstore regularly. Allow the kids to check out whatever they want, even if you find it sophomoric and immature. After all, children are immature. A trip to a bookstore can be a family adventure, and even hesitant readers usually enjoy purchasing a shiny new book of their very own.

5. Ask older kids to read to younger siblings. This will yield numerous benefits: It will improve the older child's reading skills and diction, show the younger that reading is fun for people other than adults, and encourage the two siblings to, as they say, bond.

6. Limit TV, video, and computer time. Don't be too draconian here: a house rule of no television after 8 or 9 p.m. during the school week might be sensible, with some leeway for special programs. Your goal is not to deprive the child of television so much as to make him or her indifferent to it. Ideally, evenings should be a time for reading, homework, quiet games, conversation. I know, I know: I'm a dreamer.

7. Encourage any reading interest—no matter how frivolous or unacademic you find it. If your daughter enjoys one Nancy Drew mystery, buy or check out a couple more. If she likes learning about constellations or witches or the Civil War, make sure you pick up books and pamphlets about them. As with anything, you start from where you are. The child who hunches over the Hardy Boys today will read Agatha Christie tomorrow and *Crime and Punishment* a few years after—if he or she is encouraged. The worst thing you can do is to ignore or denigrate a child's taste.

8. Don't harp on "good books." Remember how boring you thought required school reading was? Nothing kills what pleasure a novel might offer like ordering a kid to read it just because it's won a Newbery or Coretta Scott King award. Roald Dahl pointed out that what really matters in children's books is that

they be so entertaining that they "convince the child that reading is great fun."

9. Ask librarians and booksellers for advice. These professionals nearly always know what works and what doesn't.

10. Talk about books with your kids. Mention your own reading. Draw their attention to items in the Sunday paper. Ask them which is their favorite Lemony Snicket or Judy Blume title—and why.

11. Encourage kids to write. By writing stories, journals, letters, what have you, young people learn about the structure of prose, the flow of sentences, the importance of charm, and the nature of argument.

12. Take kids to meet writers at libraries and bookstores. A book becomes even more special when it's inscribed by a favorite author. On such occasions, a YA novelist can suddenly possess the glamor of a rock star or celebrity athlete.

13. Give the kids time with books. Allow them to stay up late reading, or to spend Saturday morning in bed with a novel. Boys and girls don't always need to be out and about; quiet time with a book ought to be fostered, encouraged—and not just a paltry fifteen minutes or so. Offer a plate of cookies, and the kids may settle down for a couple of hours.

HOUSEHOLD ACCOUNTS

Sylvia thought how all parents wanted an impossible life for their children—happy beginning, happy middle, happy ending. No plot of any kind. What uninteresting people would result if parents got their way.—Karen Joy Fowler

Nothing has a stronger influence psychologically on their environment, and especially on their children, than the unlived life of their parents.—C. G. Jung

A man who has been the indisputable favorite of his mother keeps for life the feeling of a conqueror, that confidence of success that often induces real success.—Sigmund Freud

It takes patience to appreciate domestic bliss; volatile spirits prefer unhappiness.—George Santayana

In *Owl Babies*—by Martin Waddell, with pictures by Patrick Benson—little Sarah and Percy and Bill are three baby owls who live in a hole in the trunk of a tree. As the book begins, "One night they woke up and their Owl Mother was GONE." Sarah tries to react intellectually: "Where's Mommy?" Percy is stunned: "Oh my goodness!" and Bill goes directly into shock: "I want my mommy!" Benson's picture of the forlorn Bill is a marvel: The little fellow looks perplexed, burdened with sorrow, a bit comic, yet still an owl. On the following pages the small white birds try to account for their mother's disappearance, but each such gambit ends with Bill repeating the primal wish of all who suffer, "I want my mommy!"

Eventually the fearful siblings cluster together on a single branch for comfort and mutual support. Then "the baby owls closed their owl eyes and wished their Owl Mother would come."

The next two facing pages carry only three short words: "AND SHE CAME." Across the full expanse of this oblong album, her wings spread wide, a full-grown brown owl swoops through the night. The next page shows us her view of three fluffs of white, hunched tight together on a tree limb. Then Waddell presents the sheer joy of the baby owls as they "flapped and they danced and they bounced up and down." This would have made a wonderful end, but Waddell doesn't stop there. The Owl Mother looks down and says, "WHAT'S ALL THE FUSS? You knew I'd come back."

At this point, any child will be smiling at this grumpy, realistic mom. Maybe you will be too—at least until remembering that for each of us there will come a time when we can wish and wish but the Owl Mother will never come back again.

WHAT DO PARENTS WANT?

All of us recognize that our childhoods were different from those of our parents. How could we not? Parents are constantly reminding their offspring of this very fact: "You kids today don't know the value of a dollar. . . . Do you and your brothers think money grows on trees? . . . All you teenagers care about are clothes. . . . There's more to life than just playing the guitar. . . .

Girls used to have a sense of modesty. . . . Boys tried to earn their father's respect."

I heard phrases like this when growing up yet, to my astonishment, find myself mouthing similar ones to my own sons. I used to assume this was something hormonal—that adults were obliged by their aging biology to look upon youth as feckless, irresponsible, and profoundly annoying. No doubt envy plays its part too. Unlike us, the young have yet to squander their lives. So we lay into them, hoping to rescue the apparent yahoos from their downward slide and somehow transform them into what they really ought to be—roughly ourselves, but better, smarter, richer.

Sadly, we grown-ups can't help these shameful desires. To feel proud of one's children—this is the drug that every parent hungers after. Only when the kids start to disappoint our expectations, as inevitably happens, do we settle for wanting them to be merely happy.

DOMESTIC UNREST

Back in the 1960s the psychologist R. D. Laing announced that the family was a machine designed to inflict insanity. After all, accusation and self-exculpation frequently seem the essential mode of familial communication. Surely, every child comes to feel, sooner or later, that his own parents and siblings have somehow been transformed into actors in a low-rent version of Eugene O'Neill's tumultuous drama of domestic unhappiness, *Long Day's Journey into Night*. Let the shouting and breast-beating, the rants and the weeping begin!

Just look at that recently popular genre, the memoir. To write a successful one it clearly helps to be born into a bad family. Drunken mothers, brutal fathers, manic-depressive brothers, drugged-out sisters, predatory uncles—such is the grim stock company of the modern reverie over childhood and youth. After all the early horror and trauma, the memoir can then close with a spiritual conversion or an intellectual epiphany. Nothing less will do. Besides, a happy childhood would sound so . . . schmaltzy.

Given all this, we should nonetheless also remember that the mass of moms and dads do their best. Every day they drive carpools, commute to work, run late to PTA meetings, wash clothes, dishes, and mud-covered goalies. They argue with teenagers who view them as necessary evils or merely the source of pocket money. When fathers and mothers look into mirrors, they see that their own once-bright faces have grown hollow-eyed and furrowed, as haggard as those of nineteenth-century dirt farmers photographed while they huddle before a sod hut in Nebraska just after the cyclone has wiped out the alfalfa crop. Staring into the gray distance, they wait for the next blow to fall. It is their children—whether aged ten, twenty, or forty—who have done this to them.

So a bit of advice to the young: Cut the old folks some slack.

SEASON'S READINGS

The Christmas season—which is also, of course, the Hanukkah and Kwanzaa season—always brings out the worst in children.

Greed, of course. But also gluttony, envy, and persistent whining. Older kids will whisper to three-year-olds that there is no Santa Claus. Brother will take up arms against brother, sister inform on sister. Interfamily poking soon grows pandemic: "He hit me." "I did not." "You started it." "No, you did." Bam, bash. Exaggerated yowls of pain. "It was his fault." "I didn't do anything." "You did." "You always blame me." "You always start it." "You're a sissy." "You're a tattletale." Meanwhile, gifts marked fragile are vigorously shaken, then dropped, then stepped on. Invariably, somebody will crash into the newly decorated tree, or slip on the ice, or be hit with a snowball. Really an ice ball. With a stone in the center.

Meanwhile, frustrated parents daydream of what the holidays are supposed to be like: neighborhood caroling on moonlit evenings, plates of star-shaped sugar cookies and mugs of steaming cocoa, Grandma reciting "A Visit from St. Nicholas," little ones, snug beneath comforters, imagining the approaching sound of reindeer hooves.

For as long as there have been holidays, there have been complaints that they have grown overly commercial and that the true spirit of the season has been forgotten. Is there nowhere known some bow or brooch or braid or brace that will help us bring back the holiday feeling we yearn for—that feeling of warmth, coziness, spiritual joy, and family happiness? Well, family reading—you saw this coming, didn't you?—can be a start. The traditional choice is *A Christmas Carol*, either in its entirety or in the version Dickens abridged for his one-man performances. Scrooge's redemption remains a powerful and moving fable, but it may be so familiar that many families hunger for other seasonal texts. Consider some of the following, whether for reading aloud or privately to refresh your own harried spirit.

1. The Gospel account of Christ's birth. Presumably Christians hear this spoken aloud during church services, yet even non-believers can appreciate the story's power and beauty. Try reading Mark or Luke's narrative at home, preferably in an English version with some grandeur to it: the King James, the Revised Standard (largely based on the King James), or even William Tyndale's early modern translation. The happy few who know the languages might even attempt the Latin Vulgate or Greek original; just hearing those ancient sounds should soothe and touch the soul.

2. John Masefield's *The Box of Delights;* Dylan Thomas's *A Child's Christmas in Wales;* the "Dulce Domum" chapter of *The Wind in the Willows;* Henry Van Dyke's "The Story of the Other Wise Man"; O. Henry's "The Gift of the Magi"; *Sir Gawain and the Green Knight.* These are holiday classics—rich with mystery and blazing fires and selfless generosity, beautifully told. Masefield's novel, a plum pudding of strange adventures, English legend, and spiritual feeling, should be more widely appreciated: During Christmas week, some devilish criminals attempt to steal a very old box, from an aged Punch-and-Judy puppeteer, who gives it to the schoolboy Kay Harker for safekeeping. Dreamlike marvels ensue. *Sir Gawain and the Green Knight*—a high point of Middle English literature—relates the surprisingly sexy tale of how Gawain travels north to face certain death at Christmas but meets

a strange and bitter destiny instead, one that leaves the proud knight thoroughly chastened.

3. Ghost stories. Victorian magazines fostered the practice of serializing shivery tales in December. The more restrained English-style ghost story is what you want this time of year, not the serial murderer with a chainsaw. I recommend *The Oxford Book of English Ghost Stories*, and any comprehensive volumes devoted to Sheridan Le Fanu (*In a Glass Darkly*), Vernon Lee (*Hauntings*), M. R. James (*Ghost Stories of an Antiquary*), Arthur Machen (*The Three Impostors*), Algernon Blackwood (*The Tales of Algernon Blackwood*), and E. F. Benson (*Spook Stories*), as well as the work of A. M. Burrage, H. R. Wakefield, Walter de la Mare, Robert Aickman, and Robert Westall. Don't overlook our North American masters, either, especially the eldritch (or kitsch) H. P. Lovecraft, the almost theological Russell Kirk (look for his powerfully emotional tale "There's a Long, Long Road A-Winding"), and the tongue-in-cheek Robertson Davies (see his cozy *High Spirits*). Individual classics like James's "Count Magnus" or Blackwood's "The Wendigo" almost demand firesides, down comforters, and mugs of mulled cider or Irish coffee.

4. Golden-age mysteries. What could be better on a chilly night than a seemingly impossible-to-solve murder, preferably in an isolated country house? Try Agatha Christie's *Murder for Christmas* and Nicholas Blake's *The Corpse in the Snowman*. Or almost anything by Rex Stout, Dorothy Sayers, or Ellery Queen. John Dickson Carr's locked-room masterpiece, *The Three Coffins*,

takes place against a backdrop of wintry weather, snug eating-places, and lots of warming drink. Of course, one of Sherlock Holmes's greatest cases, "The Blue Carbuncle"—the problem of the goose and the missing jewel—remains the ideal short Yuletide mystery. Neither should one overlook those classic authors of "true crime," William Roughead and Edmund Pearson. They possess a winey, period flavor all their own, as they describe the ancient malefactions of the "Resurrection men" Burke and Hare, the poisoner Madeleine Smith, and our own Lizzie Borden.

5. Children's stories. Christmas is primarily for children, or so they say, and there's nothing like sharing a good picture book with a young boy or girl to generate that longed-for shared seasonal contentment. Consider those wordless classics, Raymond Brigg's *The Snowman* and Peter Spier's *Christmas*, any illustrated version of Clement Moore's *A Visit from St. Nicholas* (the older the pictures the better), Russell Hoban's touching *The Mole Family's Christmas*, William Joyce's adventure-filled *Santa Calls*, Barbara Robinson's very funny novel *The Best Christmas Pageant Ever*, Chris Van Allsburg's *The Polar Express*, or the perennially popular *How the Grinch Stole Christmas* by Dr. Seuss.

6. Of course, there's a long list of sui generis holiday favorites: Max Beerbohm's perfectly pitched set of literary parodies, *A Christmas Garland*; Milton's ode "On the Morning of Christ's Nativity"; P. G. Wodehouse's hilarious "Jeeves and the Yuletide Spirit"; that gallows-humored chiller by John Collier, "Back for Christmas"; Arthur C. Clarke's disturbing science fiction minia-

ture, "The Star"; Somerset Maugham's beautifully crafted novel of lost illusions, *Christmas Holiday;* any number of Tolstoy's compassionate and inspiring parables, especially "Where Love Is, God Is"; and, not least, Damon Runyon's inimitable account of "The Three Wise Guys."

Though books can obviously help create a holiday spirit, do not neglect other traditional activities. Listen to Christmas songs on the radio. Go caroling in your neighborhood. Take in a performance of Handel's *Messiah* or Tchaikovsky's *Nutcracker.* At the least, put up a few colored lights, a wreath, maybe some holly or mistletoe. Light the candles. Bake gingerbread and sugar cookies. Help the less fortunate. Even if you don't observe Christmas, be with those you love, be festive and thankful. Rejoice.

Six

LIVING IN THE WORLD

I assure you, doctor, it is a relatively simple matter for a weathered charlatan like myself to keep up interest in so small a carnival as this.
— FRIEDRICH NIETZSCHE

TAKING THINGS LIGHTLY

According to the seventeenth-century divine Thomas Fuller, "We are born crying, live complaining, and die disappointed." In other words, life is real! life is earnest! Philosophers and moral essayists, tragic dramatists and unhappy poets all agree about this. As a consequence, the tone of most reflections on this world tends toward the meditative, melancholy, and disenchanted. Woe, woe, and more woe— it's downhill all the way, the paths of glory lead but to the grave, and stoic endurance would seem the best we can aim for. "If a man has learnt to think," says Tolstoy, "no matter what he may think about, he is always thinking of his own death."

And yet. "Unmitigated seriousness is always out of place in human affairs." counsels the philosopher George Santayana, adding, "Let not the unwary reader think me flippant for saying so; it was Plato, in his solemn old age, who said it." Certainly if there is any worldly talent worth cultivating, it's a sense of humor. To possess a cheerful outlook may be the greatest gift of the gods, the distant second best being a taste for irony. Such temperaments allow one to step back from painful situations and view them with a little detachment. Why else do we live, concluded Jane Austen, but "to make sport for our neighbours and laugh at them in return"? To the genial-spirited anything that happens can be shrugged off as yet another part of "life's rich pageant."

But how can one acquire such an upbeat attitude? In the same way we acquire all our habits—through practice. Psychologist William James discovered that if one pretended to be happy, this "going through the motions" would by itself lead to an improved mood. In other words: Act as you would like to be. It pays to picture the sort of character you present to the world. Do you want to be regarded as a whiner, a self-pitying hypochondriac, a man without backbone, a woman without pride? We all admire those who can control themselves, who—to use clichés—look on the bright side or possess a sunny disposition. The world, it's said, may be a tragedy for those who feel, but it can be a comedy, or at least a comedy of errors, for those who think.

"The most effective weapon of any man is to have reduced his share of histrionics to a minimum." This was the watchword of

André Malraux, the French novelist, adventurer, art historian, politician. Malraux believed in maturity, in being a grown-up. While our natural tendency may be to exaggerate our sorrows and fears, things often don't turn out as badly as expected. Nevertheless, we all tend to get caught up in emotional situations, carried away by our own sense of personal melodrama. In short, we overreact, indeed overact, performing for an audience, whether real or imagined. Instead of adopting such staginess, we should remind ourselves that clarity is as much a mental and emotional virtue as it is a stylistic one. Do we really feel this riot of emotion? Is there any point to all this brouhaha? Should a grown-up behave like this?

Father Anthony de Mello, a Jesuit teacher with a taste for Zen-like parables, published a series of books in which he emphasized how much our pervasive sense of unhappiness in the world arises from our attachments. For a Catholic priest he sometimes sounds positively Buddhist in his insistence that the source of emotional anguish is a "state of clinging caused by belief that without some particular thing or some person you cannot be happy." He explains in *The Way to Love* that "the tragedy of an attachment is that if its object is not attained it causes unhappiness. But if it is attained, it does not cause happiness—it merely causes a flash of pleasure followed by weariness, and it is always accompanied, of course, by the anxiety that you may lose the object of your attachment." To be genuinely happy one actually needs to rid the self of worldly entanglements. Purity and stillness, said Lao-tzu, are the correct principles for humankind.

No doubt such austerity works. And yet "what really makes one indignant about suffering isn't the thing itself but the senslessness of it." That's a sentence by Nietzsche, who endured debilitating headaches, increasing blindness, eventual insanity, and an early death. The English essayist William Hazlitt was even more explicit: "Man is the only animal that laughs and weeps; for he is the only animal that is struck with the difference between what things are, and what they ought to be." During periods of crisis somber moods return to attack even the most Falstaffian among us. Insofar as we are human, feelings of loss and regret are sometimes unavoidable, but we should remain keenly wary of overindulging them. In Benjamin Disraeli's words, "Grief is the agony of an instant: the indulgence of grief is the blunder of a life."

Easy enough to say, and we are still likely to fail at the sticking point. Yet a certain sangfroid, urbanity, or wit may be cultivated even in the face of mortal illness. A year or two before he died in his early fifties, the English critic Kenneth Tynan one afternoon detected a yellow discharge from his penis. He ruefully noted in his diary: "Bankruptcy, emphysema, paralysis of the will—and now this! Feel that God is making his point with rather vulgar overstatement."

Just writing those two sentences must have helped Tynan confront his despair, even as its unexpected humor makes a reader smile. Boethius argued for "the consolation of philosophy" and rightly too, but comic and worldly writers remind us of the "Consolation of Personal Style." We want to go out just as we lived, true to ourselves, with a quip and a blazing six-gun like Butch Cassidy and the Sundance Kid, or like James Thurber's Walter Mitty, facing his imaginary firing squad, "with that faint, fleeting smile playing about his lips."

To read Congreve, Molière, Voltaire, and Austen, or Oscar Wilde, Ronald Firbank, and Barbara Pym is to enter, for a while, a world of ease and verbal felicity. Writers like S. J. Perelman and G. K. Chesterton aren't merely humorists; they are palliatives for the human condition; sources of light and optimism. For me, in particular, P. G. Wodehouse—master of silly situations and dizzying similes—possesses the wand of the enchanter:

> "What a girl! He had never in his life before met a woman who could write a letter without a postscript, and this was but the smallest of her unusual gifts."

> "He resembled . . . in his general demeanour one of those unfortunate gentlemen in railway station waiting-rooms who, having injudiciously consented at four-thirty to hold a baby for a strange woman, looks at the clock and sees that it is now six-fifteen and no relief in sight."

> "The unpleasant, acrid smell of burnt poetry."

> "Myrtle Prosser was a woman of considerable but extremely severe beauty. She . . . suggested rather one of those engravings of the mistresses of Bourbon kings which make one feel that the monarchs who selected them must have been men of iron, impervious to fear, or else shortsighted."

THE WORLD AS IT IS

Some conjurors say that number three is the magic number, and some say number seven. It's neither, my friend, neither. It's number one.—Charles Dickens (spoken by Fagin in *Oliver Twist*)

There is a demand today for men who can make wrong appear right.—Terence

The two principal requisites in a courtier are a flexible conscience, and an inflexible politeness.—Lady Blessington

Was not the world a vast prison, and women born slaves?
—Mary Wollstonecraft

History "is all full. And dripping. With the corpses. Of them who trusted the incorruptible."—China Miéville

A horse does not understand that it has been born into the world to pull carts. It thinks it is here to be beaten. It thinks of a cart as a huge object it is tied to so that it cannot run away while it is being beaten.—J. M. Coetzee

The Washington elite is always assuring the president that "the time has come for harder choices, when the hardest choices they'd ever made, once they got through multiple choice in college, were listed on menus and wine lists."—James McCourt

In the battle between the world and you, back the world.
—Franz Kafka

BEHAVES WELL WITH OTHERS

What matters most in a civilized world? According to the philosopher Bertrand Russell, "The thing, above all that a teacher should endeavour to produce in his pupils if democracy is to survive, is the kind of tolerance that springs from an endeavour to understand those who are different from ourselves." His contemporary George Santayana made essentially the same point in reverse: "The surest way to corrupt a young man is to teach him to esteem more highly those who think alike than those who think differently." This doctrine was stated even more tellingly centuries ago by the even greater thinker Benedict Spinoza: *"Sedulo curavi humanas actiones non ridere non lugere neque detestari, sed intelligere."*—"I have laboured carefully, when faced with human actions, not to mock, not to lament, not to execrate, but to understand."

Such tolerance ranks at the top of the civic virtues. Yet some writers criticize this view as leading to a kind of situational ethics, one that precludes moral judgment or firm action. As the French say, *"Tout comprendre, c'est tout pardoner"*—to understand all is is to forgive all.

But should one? Aristotle concluded that we each remain accountable for the sort of person we are. If a man was sexually abused as a child, this may explain why he might have become an abuser as an adult, but cannot expunge his culpability: Our actions define our moral character. Carry tolerance and understanding too far, after all, and you could claim that none of our behavior is volitional, that everything is entirely conditioned, outside our control, and thus excusable.

Still, one can duly understand the historic explanations for evil and injustice without, for example, pardoning racism or the exploitation of the poor and disenfranchised. Besides, sometimes even the most righteous-seeming actions can be subtly coarsening or even morally injurious; we have heard since childhood that those who live by the sword perish by the sword and that those who sow the wind will reap the whirlwind. Heartbreakingly, in order to defeat our enemies, we have often adopted their methods. To this day the decisions to drop the atomic bombs on Hiroshima and Nagasaki, as well as the intense firebombing of German cities like Dresden, are hotly debated: Were these measures intended to end the war more quickly, or were they largely expressions of bloodlust and a desire for revenge?

We should always be exceptionally alert to any situation, political or personal, that generates a strongly emotional, hot-button reaction. No real patriot, insisted Chesterton, "would ever say, 'My country, right or wrong.' It is like saying, 'My mother, drunk or sober.'" The psychologist Georg Groddeck shrewdly remarked, "Whatever you condemn, you have done yourself," and, as Cyril Connolly knew, the man who merely fears noises as a child will hate them as an adult. More often than not, that which we find repugnant in the outside world we cannot quite acknowledge as an aspect of ourselves.

"It is my belief," said Joseph Conrad, "that no man ever understands quite his own artful dodges to escape from the grim shadow of self-knowledge." Our reflexive bent is to excuse, somehow, even our most reprehensible behavior. Self-justification, rationalization, "blaming the victim," "appropriate response"—all these, and many other phrases, are generally feints to elude the truth: We have done wrong and either wish to continue to do so, or hope to deny that we have done so.

Benjamin Franklin—the echt American moralist—long ago recognized this rationalizing side to all of us: "So convenient a thing is it to be a reasonable creature, since it enables one to find or make a reason for everything one has a mind to do." As Conrad—the author of *Lord Jim* thought a lot about moral weakness—further said, the so-called wisdom of life too often "consists in putting out of sight all the reminders of our folly, of our weakness, of our mortality, all that makes against our efficiency—the memory of our failures, the hints of our undying fears, the bodies of our dead friends."

THE USE OF FORCE

The moral essayist and activist Simone Weil made of her very life a critique of modern society. Austere and unswerving in her beliefs, she ultimately died of self-imposed malnutrition, refusing to eat more than those interned by the Nazis. Before her death, she wrote brilliantly about education, the need for roots, the religious impulse, and much else. In one of her greatest essays she analyzes *The Iliad* as what she calls "the poem of force" or "might." It opens:

> The true hero, the true subject, the center of the *Iliad* is force. Force as man's instrument, force as man's master, force before

which human flesh shrinks back. The human soul, in this poem, is shown always in its relation to force: swept away, blinded by the force it thinks it can direct, bent under the pressure of the force to which it is subjected. Those who had dreamed that force, thanks to progress, now belonged to the past, have seen the poem as a historic document; those who see that force, today as in the past, is at the center of all human history, find in the *Iliad* its most beautiful, its purest mirror.

Though force does rule much of the world, it sometimes takes on various guises, appearing as social pressure, the constricting cult of bureaucratic habit, the old excuse of "I'm just carrying out orders," Kafka's world of *The Trial* and *The Castle*. Beware of such officialism. Nearly all the theories, abstractions, hierarchies, and isms of contemporary culture tend toward the same end: to saddle people, in all their glorious and individual messiness, with simple, easy-to-read labels. That which is unique is treated as generic. And the generic, unlike the unique, is always expendable.

It's so easy to be co-opted by this kind of thinking, to sacrifice kindness and human feeling to standardized procedures and tidy regulation. "The terrifying thing is that systems grow too big for men and hold them in a satanic grip, the builders no less than the victims of the system, much as large edifices and spires, created by men's hands, tower high above us, dominate us, yet may collapse over our heads and bury us." This was said by Etty Hillesum, not long before she died in a World War II concentration camp.

Alas, all too often, as the novelist Henry de Montherlant noted, if you look back at history you find that "the world has been laid waste to ensure the triumph of conceptions that are now as dead as the men that died for them." Nationalism, religious shibboleths, racial purity—the heart sinks. Civilization, said the Spanish essayist José Ortega y Gasset, "is nothing else but the attempt to reduce force to being the last resort." We have a ways to go.

One of the reasons we should read widely is to avoid falling into the more obvious rifts of prejudice and paranoia. Shirley Jackson's famous story "The Lottery," in which murder is sanctioned by civic tradition, reminds us of how easy can be the slide into accepting as normal what is in fact utterly horrible. "There has always been a lottery." Books, by their very nature and variety, help us grow in empathy for others, in tolerance and awareness. But they should increase our skepticism as well as our humanity, for all good readers know how easy it is to misread. What counts is to stay receptive and open, to reserve judgment and try to foresee consequences, to avoid the facile conclusion and be ready to change one's mind. No matter how sure you may be of a course of action, no matter how committed to any belief, remember Oliver Cromwell's plaintive entreaty: "I beseech you, in the bowels of Christ, think it possible you may be mistaken."

HISTORY ON DEADLINE

As Terry Pratchett reminds us in one of his comic novels, "the truth will make you fret." People complain about the news, that it's "all bad," nothing but hurricanes and wars and rampant corruption and higher taxes and genocide and terrorism. Alas, this is the world, my friend. If you don't like what you read about in the paper, you need to go out and help change things for the better.

Newspapers after all aren't called heralds and beacons or even—in Youngstown, Ohio—the Vindicator for nothing. Our great dailies aim to give us the facts, to tell us the truth, and by so doing to make us think hard about society, politics, almost everything. A free press really is the greatest bastion of democracy.

That sounds corny. And, of course, newspapers sometimes fail to live up to their own ideals. (Which is why they all run correction boxes.) But people who take the daily paper, if only to glance at the headlines and catch the sports scores, or to check out new scientific breakthroughs and read the book reviews, find themselves better connected with the life of their time. The news will almost certainly make you fret. If it didn't, reporters wouldn't be doing their job. But how else can you be an informed citizen, not only of your own country but of the world?

Seven

SIGHTS AND SOUNDS

The purpose of art is not the release of a momentary ejection of adrenaline but is, rather, the gradual lifelong construction of a state of wonder and serenity.　　　　　　　—GLENN GOULD

ARTISTIC CREDOS

To interest is the first duty of art; no other excellences will ever begin to compensate for failure in this, and very serious faults will be covered by this, as by charity.—C. S. Lewis

The perfection of art is to conceal art.—Quintilian

We were put on this earth to make things.—W. H. Auden

I am only an entertainer who has understood his time.
—Pablo Picasso

My desire and my hope is to gain honor, fame, and money.
—Wolfgang Amadeus Mozart

An artist cannot do anything slovenly.—Jane Austen

A picture is—primarily—a conjunction of colored planes.
—Giotto

Art and science cannot exist but in minutely organized particulars.
—William Blake

It is not the parts that matter, it is their combination.
—Vladimir Nabokov

The trouble with me is I have no imagination.—James Joyce

A poem is never finished, it is only abandoned.—Paul Valéry

The reason why the hairs stand on end, the eyes water, the throat is constricted, the skin crawls and a shiver runs down the spine when one writes or reads a true poem is that a true poem is necessarily an invocation of the White Goddess or Muse, the Mother of All Living, the ancient power of fright and lust—the female spider or the queen-bee whose embrace is death.
—Robert Graves

A pattern of resolutions and balances and harmonizations, developed through a temporal scheme.—Cleanth Brooks (defining a poem)

Slowly now, nice neat letters; / The point is to do things well /not just to do them.
—Antonio Machado

Genuine criticism will never seek to prove but to point out.
—E. R. Curtius

Our intercourse with the dead is better than our intercourse with the living. There are only three pleasures in life pure and lasting, and all derive from inanimate things—books, pictures, and the face of nature.—William Hazlitt

The artistic temperament is a disease that afflicts amateurs.
—G. K. Chesterton

There is a moment when every work in the process of being created benefits from the glamour attaching to uncompleted sketches. 'Don't touch it any more,' cries the amateur. *It is then that the true artist takes his chance.*—Jean Cocteau

The only real voyage of discovery, the only Fountain of Youth, consists not in seeking new landscapes but in having new eyes, in seeing the universe with the eyes of another, of a hundred others, in seeing the hundred universes that each of them sees. And this we can do with a Renoir or a Debussy; with such as they we fly indeed from star to star.—Marcel Proust

"You see this important mass of colour here," the art critic Roger Fry once remarked during a lecture, indicating with his pointer the body of Christ on the cross.

THE PLEASURE PRINCIPLE

Our age, like any other, is an age of ideology, where works of art are regularly judged by their faithfulness to various political or social models. At one extreme, stern traditionalists call for a return to a high Victorian curriculum, based on the age-old classics, the melancholy, no-nonsense wisdom of Samuel Johnson and a pious Arnoldian seriousness about literature as a corrective to life. At the other extreme, tenured professors gaily announce that books are outmoded and we should be studying, with the devotion of Talmudic scholars, "reality" TV programs, biker magazines, and rap lyrics.

There are some thinkers who maintain that everyone is right, that art and literature thrive on just this conflict and excess and abundance. Dialectic is a sign of health. To further adopt a pseudo-Hegelian perspective, we should welcome the work of previously marginalized groups, not because to do so is "fair" but because by integrating their work into the canon, art as a whole is reinvigorated, enlarged, made new again. How else can we keep things fresh and exciting?

Still, there remains another view, whose advocate is Walter Pater (1839–94). Usually called "art for art's sake," Pater's aesthetic doctrine might be better described as "art for my sake." In a series of essays, collected in books like *The Renaissance*, *Appreciations*, and *Imaginary Portraits*, this shy, retiring Oxford don—plain of face, homosexual, and heterodox in his religious beliefs—proposed that the purpose of art is simply to give personal pleasure. Painting, poetry, and music don't teach us moral lessons or make us better citizens. No, they enrich our all-too-brief lives by investing each moment with the highest quality. Through art we may not live any longer, but we can live better, more intensely. As one of Pater's best-known purple patches has it: "Not the fruit of experience, but experience itself, is the end. A counted number of pulses only is given to us of a variegated, dramatic life. How may we see in them all that is to be seen in them by the finest senses? How shall we pass most swiftly from point to point, and be present always at the focus where the greatest number of vital forces unite in their purest energy? To burn always with this hard, gemlike flame, to maintain this ecstasy, is success in life."

That's from the postscript to *The Renaissance*. In its preface Pater impudently defines the essential critical act: "What is this song or picture, this engaging personality presented in life or in a book, to me? What effect does it really produce on me? Does it give me pleasure? And if so, what sort or degree of pleasure?"

For Pater the function of aesthetic education must be to create "a certain kind of temperament, the power of being deeply moved by the presence of beautiful objects." Yet he insists one should "remember always that beauty exists in many forms" and that "all periods, types, schools of taste, are in themselves equal." In an era that emphasized socially responsible, at times almost civic art (among writers, think of John Ruskin, George Eliot, Matthew Arnold), the timid Pater was deeply subversive, his antinomian instincts calling always for more freedom, passion, and delight. He is, after all, the man who looked to the Renaissance as a time of "brilliant sins and exquisite amusements." Against the strictures of his own moralizing age, he maintained that the wider, deeper, and more various our aesthetic sympathies, the richer will be our lives at every moment.

THE SHOCK OF THE NEW

People who live near the seashore no longer hear the waves. Our senses are deadened by the routine and quotidian. Art, though, makes the familiar strange again, so that it can be freshly perceived. This necessary "defamiliarization" or "enstrangement"— to use terms coined in the 1920s by a group of critics called the Russian formalists—explains why true art often appears outlandish, disturbing, grotesque, or very, very puzzling: It is trying to break through the automatization of our dulled response to the world around us. The novelist's task, as Joseph Conrad famously said, is simply "to make you see."

Artists have long recognized this need for ambitious work to eschew the cozy and soothing, the expected approach, the conventionally beautiful. This isn't simply a twentieth-century philosophy of shocking the bourgeoisie. "There is no excellent beauty that hath not some strangeness in the proportion," said Francis Bacon in the time of Queen Elizabeth I, just as critic Harold Bloom asserted, in the time of Elizabeth II, that "when you read a canonical work for a first time you encounter a stranger, an uncanny startlement rather than a fulfillment of expectations." Writing halfway between both, Goethe observed much the same: "All great excellences in life or art, at its first recognition, brings with it a certain pain arising from the strongly felt inferiority of the spectator; only at a later period, when we take it into our own culture, and appropriate as much of it as our own capacities allow, do we learn to love and esteem it. Mediocrity, on the other hand, may often give us unqualified pleasure; it does not disturb one's self-satisfaction, but rather encourages us with the thought that we are as good as another."

The innovative, then, needs time to be explored and understood. "Great masterpieces," said Proust, "do not disappoint us by giving us their best first." And so when you attend a concert or visit a gallery and are confronted by what seems to you ugly or upsetting or incomprehensible, be hesitant about giving it an instant thumbs-down. Yes, the painting may look as if your third grader did it in Day-Glo crayon, the concert sound nothing like Mozart or the Beatles, and yet, just maybe, you are missing the point. *The Rite of Spring* provoked a riot; Jackson Pollock's abstractions were dismissed as jokes. Which of us would have immediately recognized their originality and grandeur? Wait awhile. Only critics on deadline must rush to judgment. I like the philosopher Arthur Schopenhauer's modest advice: "We should comport ourselves with the masterpieces of art as with exalted personages—stand quietly before them and wait till they speak to us."

BUT IS IT ART?

In 1878 the influential critic, prose stylist, and social visionary John Ruskin attacked James McNeill Whistler for trying to foist off slapdash daubs as works of art and so hoodwink the ignorant public. The painter sued for libel, and the case went to court.

In the most famous exchange during the trial a lawyer snidely asked Whistler, "How long do you take to knock off one of your pictures?" The artist answered that it had taken him one or two days "to knock off" his *Nocturne in Black and Gold: The Falling Rocket*, a blurry night-scene of the Thames, painted in shades of black, with a few flashes of color from fireworks. Then came the crucial question. Lawyer: "The labor of two days is that for which you ask two hundred guineas?" Whistler: "No, I ask it for the knowledge I have gained in the work of a lifetime."

Though Ruskin was required to pay a derisory sum in damages, nothing was truly resolved by the trial. The far-reaching debate about the value of art goes on to this day. Does art have a social or moral function? Or is it autonomous? Does it need to be pleasing? (In his last Slade lectures Ruskin wildly overpraised the saccharine children's illustrations of Kate Greenaway.) Or should it shake us as profoundly as possible, like the "Black" paintings of Goya (e.g., *Cronos Devouring His Children*) or the sadomasochistic photographs of Robert Mapplethorpe? Who can properly judge a contemporary work— only another artist? a critic? the public? the marketplace? Is criticism simply a branch of rhetorical persuasiveness? ("The true work of a critic," said Ruskin, "is not to make his hearer believe him, but agree with him.") In sum, how does one determine value, whether monetary or aesthetic? (At first no one would buy *The Falling Rocket*; years later Whistler sold it for eight hundred guineas; today it is a treasure of the Detroit Institute of Arts.)

Whistler's viewpoint—that art possesses its own inherent form and beauty outside any anecdotal qualities, social concerns, or traditional expectations—harmonizes with received doctrines of high modernism. But why bother with art if it has little or no relationship to life? Because it does, and must. In more recent years an artwork's often unexpressed ideologies, whether political, social, or sexual, have again obsessed academic critics. The pendulum swings, the questions continue.

Once an acolyte came up to Ruskin to tell him how much he enjoyed his writings. "I don't care whether you enjoyed them," shot back the social prophet and moralist, "did they do you any good?" When a similarly enthusiastic admirer compared Whistler to the great Spanish portraitist Velázquez, the creator of *The White Girl* (in the National Gallery) and *The Peacock Room* (at the Freer) replied with his own typical modesty, "Why drag in Velázquez?"

You pay your money and you take your choice. Ultimately, of course, what matters most isn't simply plumping for one view over the other, but thinking and arguing about the issues raised. By so doing, each of us comes to understand more fully the place of art in our own lives. So look hard, listen closely, and strive, as Henry James urged, to "be one on whom nothing is lost."

VISUAL ACUITY

The writer Jeanette Winterson once asked a friend who had a good cellar how she could learn about wine. "Drink it," he said. This advice is true of all the arts: To learn about music, listen to it, to learn about art, look at it.

Art books, especially those sumptuous *grandes horizontales* of the coffee table, are no substitute for actual paintings, prints, and drawings. After all, only the work of art itself is art; everything else is a copy, merely a pictorial aide-mémoire. By its very nature, then, a *Paintings in the Hermitage*, for example, can be only a very big collection of postcards, albeit quite large ones, reminding us of the glories in store for the visitor to Russia. It is usually far better to spend an hour at the nearest museum than an evening looking at color reproductions. But once we've found ourselves drawn to the work of Bronzino or Brancusi, or discovered a passion for seventeenth-century Dutch landscapes, we can turn to monographs or albums. Art first, then art books.

Still, anyone who is interested in the visual arts will gather about him or her a small library of critical and scholarly texts. Obviously, there are standard catalogues raisonnés for every major painter and movement, and the person who reveres, say, Watteau will want the specialized studies of Donald Posner and Michael Levey, as well as the fat exhibition volume of the Watteau extravaganza mounted by the National Gallery of Art. But there are more general histories and nontechnical works directed toward the novice art lover and occasional visitor to the concert hall and theater. Setting aside music, which is covered in the next section, here's a very basic starter kit. Nearly all these books can be enjoyed for their prose and the strong personalities of their authors as well as for their insights on their respective subjects:

James Agee, *On Film*
Kenneth Clark, *Civilisation; Looking at Pictures*
Edwin Denby, *Looking at the Dance; Dance Writings*
Ernst Gombrich, *Art and Illusion*
Robert Hughes, *Nothing If Not Critical*
William Ivins, Jr., *How Prints Look*
H. W. Janson, *History of Art*
Pauline Kael, *I Lost It at the Movies; Deeper into Movies*
Michael Levey, *Early Renaissance; High Renaissance*
André Malraux, *The Voices of Silence*
Bernard Shaw, *Dramatic Opinions and Essays*
Kenneth Tynan, *Curtains; Tynan Right and Left; Show People*
Giorgio Vasari, *Lives of the Most Excellent Sculptors, Painters and Architects*

HEARD MELODIES

All the arts, famously proclaimed Walter Pater, "constantly aspire to the condition of music." For not only is music the purest of the arts, this daughter of Mnemosyne is also the most powerful: With his lyre Orpheus could persuade trees to walk and the king of the

Underworld to release the dead. Before Copernicus wrecked everything, people even knew that the sun, stars, and planets were pushed about by angels and that their progress through the sky created the celestial harmony of the spheres.

Today, most concertgoers turn to music for emotion, to feel a rush of exaltation or a pang of melancholy; what Santayana called "a drowsy reverie relieved by nervous thrills." Wallace Stevens says this more beautifully (in the poem "Peter Quince at the Clavier"): "Just as my fingers on these keys/ Make music, so the selfsame sounds / On my spirit make a music too. / So music is feeling then, not sound."

But to progress beyond mere passive listening, one can at least start by reading some of the more accessible writing about classical music. Classical music? Let me point out that, like many people, I love jazz and popular song and some rock, but in a wholly sentimental fashion, while I believe the work of Bach, Mozart, and Wagner delivers a deeper and more enduring satisfaction. Still, it's "strange how potent cheap music is," as Noel Coward rather dismissively remarked, and I can come close to tears over oldies and country-and-western heartbreakers. I also know that Louis Armstrong, Charlie Parker, and Miles Davis created enduring and serious masterpieces, and that there are times when a person needs to listen to Art Tatum, Antonio Carlos Jobim, or Billie Holiday. They are amazing artists. In the end, though, no matter what you turn to on the radio or CD player, Nietzsche certainly seems to have gotten it right: "Without music life would be a mistake."

It's hard, even impossible, to convey the experience of sound through words, especially to a general reader without much knowledge of composition and theory. So most of us turn to introductory guides, biographies, and collections of reviews.

Luckily, many of our best musical commentators have been lively prose stylists. Pianist Glenn Gould offered radio shows in which he displayed both his convictions and his wit: "One does not play the piano with one's fingers, one plays the piano with one's mind." The famously eccentric Canadian once imagined a fictional musicologist and avant-garde composer Karlheinz Klopweisser, whose interests included "the resonance of silence," specifically "German silence, which is of course organic, as opposed to French silence, which is ornamental."

The conductor and polymath Robert Craft worked as Igor Stravinsky's assistant, adviser, and confidant for many years. His encounters with the Russian master—recorded in the diarylike *Stravinsky: Chronicle of a Friendship* and a half dozen volumes of conversations—can be as lively as Boswell's life of Johnson. After all, Stravinsky knew, and sometimes worked closely with, such varied artistic giants as Rodin, Debussy, Diaghilev, Picasso, Mann, Valéry, Cocteau, Auden, and Disney. Even Joyce and Proust once attended the same soiree in Stravinsky's honor. (Of course, this sort of thing is hardly unusual for a great musician: On a single stroll down a Paris boulevard in 1840, the composer Liszt ran into Heine, Balzac, Chopin, and Berlioz.)

Nicolas Slonimsky's *Baker's Biographical Dictionary of Musicians* is a mammoth reference book suffused with its compiler's wry personality. Consider Slonimsky's entry on himself, which blithely opens, "A legendary Russian-born American musicologist of manifold endeavors" and goes on: "Possessed by inordinate ambition, aggravated by the endemic intellectuality of his family on both maternal and paternal branches (novelists, revolutionary poets, literary critics, university professors, translators, chessmasters, economists, mathematicians, inventors of useless artificial languages, Hebrew scholars, speculative philosophers), he became determined to excel beyond common decency in all these doctrines."

Slonimsky, like Robert Craft in his own critical work, is a ravenous intellectual magpie whose several books on music spill over with odd, believe-it-or-not facts. A poet named Schubart, we learn, was "the author of the words of *Die Forelle* by Schubert." The eccentric composer Kaikhosru Sorabji lives in a castle in Dorset with this sign on his gatepost: "Visitors Unwelcome. Roman Catholic Nuns in Full Habit May Enter without an Appointment." In his *Lexicon of Musical Invective* Slonimsky notes that an early reviewer of Stravinsky dubbed his most famous work "Le Massacre du Printemps." Another called Debussy's masterpiece "La Mal de Mer." Nearly always subtly playful, Slonimsky does know when to pull out all the stops. J. S. Bach's entry in *Baker's* begins with this resounding organ roll: "Supreme arbiter and lawgiver of music, a master comparable in greatness of stature with Aristotle in philosophy and Leonardo da Vinci in art."

The three volumes of George Bernard Shaw's collected musical criticism can be enjoyed for the sharpness of its author's convictions (Shaw was a "perfect Wagnerite" and couldn't grasp Schumann, Brahms, or Dvořák) and for the pleasure of his pungent expression—GBS once remarked that he could make tired stockbrokers read his reviews. And they did. "A readable unfavorable notice is a better advertisement than an unreadable or at any rate unmemorable puff." He was best in humorous attack: The "fiddlers rambled from bar to bar with a sweet indecision that had a charm of its own, but was not exactly what Purcell and Handel meant."

At his own best, the highly opinionated B. H. Haggin was nearly Shaw's American counterpart: "It is the capacity for making good or bad art a personal matter that makes a man a critic." Haggin adopted a kind of New Critical approach to music, focusing his attention strictly on what he heard with his own ears, utterly disdaining received opinion. He was absolutely self-confident about his draconian judgments (and, not surprisingly, grew querulous and paranoid in his old age). His *Music for One Who Enjoys Hamlet* and *New Listener's Musical Companion* remain among the most exhilarating and provocative introductions to classical music ever written.

Composers themselves have often brought out first-rate musical commentary. Think of Hector Berlioz's *Evenings in the Orchestra* or Claude Debussy's writings as Monsieur Croche, the dilettante hater. In the United States we can look to such masters as Leonard Bernstein, Aaron Copland, Virgil Thomson, and Ned Rorem, all of whom produced essays and books for a general audience. Thomson and Rorem are my own favorites.

In the early 1970s I bought a used paperback (seventy-five cents) of Thomson's *Music Reviewed: 1940–1954* in a ramshackle bookshop near the bus station in Oneonta, New York. (It became one of my sacred texts, up there with William Empson's *Seven Types of Ambiguity* and Randall Jarrell's *Poetry and the Age*.) Early in the book Thomson blasts the then revered Vladimir Horowitz as not so much a virtuoso as a showman: "He is out to wow the public, and wow it he does. He makes a false accent or phrasing anywhere he thinks it will attract attention." The roly-poly Thomson, who worked with Gertrude Stein (*Four Saints in Three Acts*) and knew James Joyce, was also a superb letter writer: "I did not notice the misprint 'Angus Dei.' Theologically the cow might as well have been adopted by the Deity as the lamb. Both are peaceful beasts." In a beautifully mean epigram, Thomson once compared composers Elliott Carter and Aaron Copland in the role of Great Man: "When Aaron reached the top, at least he sent the elevator back down."

Thomson's longer essays on music are just as thoughtfully amusing. Take this passage from *Music Right and Left:*

> If a lady of means really wants an artistic husband, a composer is about the best bet, I imagine. Painters are notoriously unfaithful, and they don't age gracefully. They dry up and sour. Sculptors are of an incredible stupidity. Poets are either too violent or too tame, and terrifyingly expensive. Also, due to the exhausting nature of their early lives, they are likely to be impotent after forty. Pianists and singers are megalomaniacs; conductors worse. Besides, executants don't stay home enough. The composer, of all art-workers in the vineyard, has the prettiest manners and ripens the most satisfactorily. His intellectual and his amorous powers seldom give out completely before death. His musical powers not uncommonly increase.

In our own day, Ned Rorem is nearly as famous for his youthful "amorous powers" as for his music. (He has been generally acclaimed as our leading composer of art-song.) Once an enfant terrible and now a grand old man, Rorem is worldly, witty, a confirmed Francophile, and deliciously immodest, in both his witty diaries and waspish criticism. Once when recalling Georges Auric's music for Jean Cocteau's *Orphée*, he punned (think *Hamlet*), "Alas, poor Auric." He notoriously acclaimed Paul McCartney and John Lennon as serious composers. Above all, he gossips wonderfully well: The composer Francis Poulenc "never chased . . . pretty boys. . . . Poulenc's taste ran to overweight gendarmes with handlebar mustaches and to middle-aged businessmen. Governor Thomas E. Dewey, Poulenc once told me, was his ideal." Just the titles of Rorem's "best of" collections suggest his verbal astringency: *Setting the Tone* and *Settling the Score*.

DESERT ISLAND DISCS

What follows is a baker's dozen of classic works of music that everyone should know. It was wrenching to leave out so much— Thomas Tallis's *Spem in Alium*, Haydn's joyful London symphonies, operas as wonderful as Monteverdi's *Orfeo*, Verdi's *Otello*, and Benjamin Britten's *Billy Budd*, Samuel Barber's haunting *Knoxville: Summer of 1915*, and even such warhorses as Dvořák's Cello Concerto and Sibelius's Second Symphony. Still, the masterpieces below are just that—timeless and inexhaustible.

1. Bach, *The Goldberg Variations* (Glenn Gould, 1981)
2. Mozart, *The Marriage of Figaro* (Rene Jacobs)
3. Mozart, *Don Giovanni* (Carlo Maria Giulini)

4. Beethoven, *Late String Quartets* (Vegh Quartet)
5. Beethoven, *Fourth Piano Concerto* (Leon Fleischer, George Szell)
6. Berlioz, *Symphonie Fantastique* (Colin Davis)
7. Schubert, *Winterreise* (Fischer-Dieskau/Moore)
8. Wagner, *Tristan und Isolde* (Wilhelm Furtwängler)
9. Stravinsky, *Le Sacre du Printemps* (Igor Stravinsky)
10. Debussy, solo piano music (*Images*, *Préludes*, etc.) (Walter Gieseking)
11. Bernstein, *Candide* (Leonard Bernstein)
12. Ella Fitzgerald, *The Complete Ella Fitzgerald Song Books* (Fitzgerald/Nelson Riddle)
13. Compilation disc of ballads, torch songs, and standards: "Smoke Gets in Your Eyes," (sung by the Platters); "Cry Me a River," (Julie London); "Maybe It Was Memphis" (Pam Tillis); "I Was the One" (Jimmie Dale Gilmore); "Somewhere over the Rainbow" (Eva Cassidy); "The Way You Look To-night" (Margaret Whiting).

And, sigh, many others.

Eight

THE INTERIOR LIBRARY

There are books . . . which rank in our life with parents and lovers and passionate experiences.   —RALPH WALDO EMERSON

READ AT WHIM!

The world is a library of strange and wonderful books, and sometimes we just need to go prowling through the stacks. Those journeys, with their serendipitous discoveries and misguided side trips, allow us to probe our characters, indulge our passions and prejudices, and finally choose books for which we possess a real affinity. Why turn, with wan languor, the pages of the current Brand Name Author when you might grow truly excited by the work of Jean Toomer or Jean Stafford, Djuna Barnes or Jeanette Winterson?

So why are people in general so sheepish, so lemminglike when it comes to the books they will spend hours with? The best seller list deserves much of the blame, because too many of us simply follow its imperious and arcane dictates. Rather than visiting a bookshop or library, rather than actually picking up a new novel or biography and skimming a few pages, we automatically buy the latest hot or fashionable title.

The best seller list tends to distort the character of entire genres. Mention fantasy, for example, and the world thinks elves, magic swords, quests, and Tolkien rip-offs, often set down in a language the likes of which was never heard on land or sea. Similarly, science fiction means *Star Wars* tie-ins or bloated works of space opera. But, as with crime fiction (Ruth Rendell, Patricia Highsmith, K. C. Constantine), true artists work in these fields, and they should be better known. Read Ursula Le Guin's *The Left Hand of Darkness*, Gene Wolfe's *Book of the New Sun*, Jack Vance's *The Dying Earth*, or Jonathan Carroll's *The Land of Laughs*. For many readers, these are already established American classics. None of these authors produces the kind of prose only an engineer could love.

If we undercut the hegemony of the fashionable, people might be more willing to try older books from the past. As the Victorian man of letters Samuel Butler observed, "The oldest books are still only just out to those who have not read them." In a sensible world, those of us with a yen for chills wouldn't simply read Stephen King; we'd also slaver over the strange stories of Robert Aickman and the haunting ones of Vernon Lee. One of the ancient goals of criticism was called the correction of taste. No one should grow world-weary thinking that John le Carré alone defines the British spy thriller, not in a century that has also produced John Buchan, Eric Ambler, Geoffrey Household, Michael Innes, Len Deighton, and Ian Fleming. But when was the last time you heard anybody talking about Ambler's *A Coffin for Dimitrios* or Household's *Rogue Male*?

Consider major works of intellectual history written in the 1990s. Richard Fletcher's *The Barbarian Conversion*, John Hale's *The Civilization of Europe in the Renaissance*, Peter Conrad's *Modern Times, Modern Places*, Peter Washington's *Madame Blavatsky's Baboon: A History of the Mystics, Mediums, and Misfits Who Brought Spiritualism to America*, and John Brewer's study of eighteenth-century England, *The Pleasures of the Imagination*—all proffer the same sort of engaging anecdotes and easygoing didacticism we associate with Dava Sobel's *Longitude*. But these more substantial books go largely unnoticed because they are judged too scholarly, too ambitious, too long. Rather than cutely packaged, bite-sized finger food, these histories spread out like holiday smorgasbords. Think tomes, not totes. Yet anybody who enjoys a best-selling charmer like Simon Winchester's *The Professor and the Madman* would certainly revel in Charles Nicholl's *The Reckoning*, a suspenseful historical reconstruction of the murder of Christopher Marlowe.

How can the ordinary reader find out about such work? Look through the review sections of newspapers and magazines. Talk to friends about their favorite books. Whenever you meet someone in an interesting profession, ask him or her about the important works in that field or the best introduction to it. Check out the acknowledgments, blurbs, and bibliographies of books you like. The historian Anthony Grafton led at least one reader to Frances Yates's literally marvel-filled *Giordano Bruno and the Hermetic Tradition* and *The Art of Memory*. Essay collections are often useful: John Updike's several capacious volumes offer introductions to writers both celebrated and neglected. There's even a whole sub-genre of books about books, from Clifton Fadiman's *Lifetime Reading Plan* to his daughter Anne Fadiman's *Ex Libris*. And, of course, the Internet offers an ever-changing array of blogs, author Web sites, Listservs, and online chats. Most of all, though, just go to libraries and bookstores. Browse. Make such visits a regular part of your life. Ask for guidance, or be adventurous. Trust your instincts, not fashion, and, to paraphrase the poet Philip Sidney: Look in thy heart and read!

PERILS OF FICTION

Most serious novels are machines for producing anxiety. Pick up a classic or a current best seller, and you'll find people in trouble: At the very least marriages break up, serial killers strike, World War III threatens. What, we wonder, will happen next—and to whom? We riffle through the pages with, as reviewers used to say, our pulses racing, stomachs in knots, hearts pounding.

Profound emotion is upsetting; it overturns our lives, uses up our psychic energies and defenses, leaving us vulnerable and more tenderly sensitive to the shocks of life. Well, almost none of us *enjoys* feeling as though we've just been batted around like a tetherball.

Yet this is what most serious novels aim to do, and why we sometimes have to steel ourselves to crack one open.

In fact, the rapport between a reader and his or her book is almost like that between lovers. The relationship grows, envelops a life, lays out new prospects and ways of seeing oneself and the future, is filled with moments of joy and sorrow; when it's over, even its memory enriches as few experiences can. But just as one cannot psychically afford to fall in love too many times, suffer its gantlet of emotions too often and still remain whole, so the novel-reader cannot read too many books of high purpose and harrowing dimension or do so too often. Burnout, a failure to respond with the intensity literature demands, is the result. As with a love affair, the battered heart needs time to recover from a good work of fiction.

This is why rereading is so important. Once we know the plot and its surprises, we can appreciate a book's artistry without the usual confusion and sap flow of emotion, content to follow the action with tenderness and interest, all passion spent. Rather than surrender to the story or the characters—as a good first reader ought—we can now look at how the book works, and instead of swooning over it like a besotted lover begin to appreciate its intricacy and craftsmanship. Surprisingly, such dissection doesn't murder the experience. Just the opposite: Only then does a work of art fully live. As Oscar Wilde once said, if a book isn't worth reading over and over again, it isn't worth reading at all. That's a bit extreme—there's a place for the never-to-be-repeated fling—but essentially he's right. This is why *Hamlet, Persuasion,* and *Abalom, Absalom!* are endlessly rereadable, why teachers look forward to discussing them year after year. Major works of the imagination only gradually disclose the various facets of their artistry; only slowly do they reveal the subtleties of their construction. The great books are those we want to spend our lives with because they never cease to reward our devotion.

FIVE PROPOSITIONS ABOUT POETRY

1. In a very general sense, poets tend to use language in two ways: the artful or the natural. Either they transmute their thoughts through metaphor, striking imagery, or unusual syntax into something rich and strange; or they pack their meaning into what Wordsworth famously called the language really used by men (and women). On the one hand, Wallace Stevens, Gerard Manley Hopkins, and Jorie Graham; on the other, William Carlos Williams, Archilochos, and Billy Collins. Most poets opt for flash and filigree—after all, "O, for a beaker full of the warm South, / Full of the true, the blushful Hippocrene" (Keats) sounds like poetry. It takes real confidence, and sure judgment, to set down words as simple and deeply moving as "Pray, undo this button" (Shakespeare).

2. Where a "Complete Poems" is a monument, a "Selected Poems" is an invitation, a sometimes needed icebreaker for shy new readers. In other words, most of us. Just as expository prose generally aims to ingratiate, emphasizing clarity and communication, so a lot of poetry blithely ignores the ordinary courtesies: It is simply there, true to itself. Let me be fanciful: If you picture good prose as a smooth politician deftly reaching out to the crowd and

welcoming everyone into the party, then poetry is Clint Eastwood, serape flapping in the wind, standing quietly alone on a dusty street, pure coiled energy. He's not glad-handing anybody.

3. To read a volume of poetry is to enter the world of the mesmerist. In a serious artist's collected poems, the single constant is usually his or her distinctive, increasingly hypnotic voice. Without relying on plot, dramatic action, or a cast of characters, lyric poets, especially, must entrance us with their words until we cannot choose but hear. Eager for more, we turn page after page because we find ourselves in thrall to a particular diction.

4. Nearly everyone can come up with good explanations for why they don't keep up with contemporary poetry, but the main one is simply that reading strange and unfamiliar poems sounds a lot like schoolwork. The language often seems so . . . high-pitched and bizarre or just plain hard to understand. In fact, the best way to enjoy contemporary verse is simply to read it as though you were dipping into a magazine, listening to a news report, overhearing a conversation. Don't make it a big deal, simply thrill to the words or story. As the critic Marvin Mudrick once proclaimed: "You don't read for understanding, you read for excitement. Understanding is a product of excitement." Later on, you can return to the poems that speak most strongly to you and make them a part of your life.

5. Memorize the poems you love most. As Anthony Burgess wrote: "The dragging out from memory of lines from *Volpone* or

The Vanity of Human Wishes with the twelfth glass is the true literary experience. I mean that. Verse is for learning by heart, and that is what a literary education should mostly consist of." When I was a teenager, I used to walk to high school. To pass those tedious twenty or thirty minutes I decided to memorize favorite lines and stanzas from Oscar Williams's anthology, *Immortal Poems of the English Language*. "With rue my heart is laden. . . . I met a traveller from an antique land. . . . We'd rather have the iceberg than the ship. . . . The waste remains, the waste remains and kills. . . . That dolphin-torn, that gong-tormented sea. . . . Our revels now are ended." In all my life no time has ever been better spent.

CREATIVE NONFICTION

There's more to literature than fiction, drama, and poetry. Here are sixteen superlatively entertaining and artful works of literary nonfiction, some of which should be better known. To narrow a wide field, I've focused on twentieth-century writers in English and arranged them in loosely chronological order.

1. Lytton Strachey, *Eminent Victorians*. Polished, witty, and ironic accounts of four pillars of nineteenth-century England, including Florence Nightingale. Strachey transformed biography from the marmoreal "life and works" to the artful portrait.

2. A. J. A. Symons, *The Quest for Corvo*. Not only a biography of Corvo, a decadent writer of the 1890s, but an account of how

Symons researched his life: the eccentrics he met, the gossip he was told, the archival materials he unearthed. Symons made Corvo's biography personal—he might even be the forgotten founder of New Journalism—and portrayed himself as a literary detective.

3. Robert Byron, *The Road to Oxiana*. Acclaimed for its originality and importance as *The Waste Land* of travel writing: two young Brits and their misadventures in the Middle East. "Water is the main difficulty of such a journey, as sufferers from syphilis of the throat, who are numerous, are apt to choose the wells to spit in."

4. Joseph Mitchell, *Up in the Old Hotel*. The finest "New Yorker profiles" of them all—wistful, poetic, and bristling with life. The subjects? Street-corner preachers, patrons of McSorley's saloon, gypsies, Mohawk Indians, watermen, and people who live in caves.

5. Isak Dinesen, *Out of Africa*. "I had a farm in Africa, at the foot of the Ngong Hills." So opens what is for many the most beautiful memoir of the century.

6. M. F. K. Fisher, *The Art of Eating*. Our most sensuous writer on food—and France and love and what one might call the Mediterranean pleasures of life.

7. Cyril Connolly, *The Unquiet Grave*. Abandoned by his wife as World War II begins, a moody, introspective man of letters reflects on failure, literary masterpieces, the function of civilization,

and his memories of the past. "I regard the burning of the Alexandrian library as an inconsolable private grief."

8. Northrop Frye, *Anatomy of Criticism*. How is literature structured? Encyclopedic in range and packed with startling insights—a work of criticism to reread just for the prose and the wonderful clarity of its author's intelligence.

9. Ivan Morris, *The World of the Shining Prince*. An enthralling introduction to a strange and beautiful world: medieval Japan and the society described in the great Japanese novel *The Tale of Genji*, where what matters are *myabi*, or courtly beauty and elegance, and *aware*, a sensitivity to the "tears in things."

10. S. Schoenbaum, *Shakespeare's Lives*. How have critics, biographers, crackpots, and readers constructed or imagined Shakespeare's life? A capacious masterpiece of entertaining scholarship, written with gusto, authority, and low-keyed humor.

11. Richard Ellmann, *James Joyce*. The finest literary biography of the twentieth century, and the best general introduction to the life and work of the Irish genius who gave us *Ulysses*.

12. Alison Lurie, *V. R. Lang: A Memoir*. Early in her career, Lurie composed this memoir as a tribute to a playwright friend who died young, and the result is a delicious account of the literary world of Harvard and Cambridge in the early 1950s. Look for cameos of the young Edward Gorey and John Ashbery, among others.

13. Bruce Chatwin, *In Patagonia*. The most influential travel book of our time. A young Englishman not only explores a romantic and forbidding country but also creates a haunting mood-piece in ninety-seven short chapters, each built on stark yet perfect sentences.

14. Truman Capote, *In Cold Blood*. The murder of a Kansas family and its aftermath, retold as a "nonfiction novel." Capote's style, reportorial genius, and hard work produced the first masterpiece of New Journalism.

15. Guy Davenport, *The Geography of the Imagination*. Scholar, translator, teacher, poet, and short-fiction writer, Davenport was superlative as all these, but utterly breathtaking in his wide-ranging essays about primitive culture, modernism, and innovative work in all the arts. Literature "is a complex dialogue of books talking to books."

16. The *Paris Review* "Writers at Work" collections (especially the first four). Conversations with William Faulkner, T. S. Eliot, Marianne Moore, Ezra Pound, and many others. These interviews established a new subgenre, providing inspiring insights into the literary life. Ernest Hemingway: "I rewrote the ending to *A Farewell to Arms*, the last page of it, thirty-nine times before I was satisfied."

ON CRITICS AND REVIEWERS

In 1557 Girolamo Cardano, notes the historian Anthony Grafton, "became the object of the most savage book review in the bitter annals of literary invective. Julius Caesar Scaliger . . . devoted more than nine hundred quarto pages to refuting one of Cardano's books, *On Subtlety*." Grafton adds that this may be "the only book review ever known to undergo transformation into a textbook."

W. H. Auden once wrote about some of his favorite book reviews, all imaginary, citing in particular several made up by the British humorist J. B. Morton. For instance, *No Second Churning*, by Arthur Clawes is "an almost unbearably vital study of a gas-inspector who puts gas-inspecting before love. Awarded the Prix de Seattle, this book should enhance the author's growing reputation as an interpreter of life's passionate bypaths." *Brittle Galaxy* is aptly described as "1,578 pages of undiluted enthrallment." Those last two words, of course, sum up what all authors want to hear said about their work.

Why is it so hard to talk—not write but speak—about art and literature? A friend asks about a new novel or collection of poetry? Almost any response tends to sound at least faintly prissy, hokey, pretentious, academic, or utterly banal.

The most typical character flaw of the bookish is the desire to show off. Many years ago I knew a kindhearted, vastly well-read guy who liked to bring up rather esoteric titles in conversation. Mentioning, say, Mervyn Peake's *Gormenghast* trilogy, he'd pause for a moment, just to see if the name registered. If, by chance, you exclaimed, "Oh, I just adore Peake's writing" and started chattering away about Steerpike and Titus Groan and the burning of the castle library, my learned friend, slightly irked, would lose all interest— and then casually allude to some other difficult, possibly even more obscure book. Did you know Thomas Mann's *Doctor Faustus*? Well, not precisely; *The Magic Mountain*, of course, but somehow—At which point, happy again, this encyclopedic autodidact would shift into high gear: "Oh yes, *The Magic Mountain*, quite a good book, one that everyone reads and should read. But *Doctor Faustus* is the real masterpiece," and away he'd go, secure in the knowledge that you were ignorant of Mann's truest and most demanding chef d'oeuvre.

What makes for a good book review? H. L. Mencken insisted that "a book review, first and foremost, must be entertaining. By this I mean that it must be dexterously written, and show an interesting personality. The justice of the criticism embodied in it is a secondary matter. It is often, and perhaps usually, quite impossible to determine definitely whether a given book is 'good' or 'bad.' The notion to the contrary is a delusion of the defectively intelligent. It is almost always accompanied by moral passion. But a critic may at least justify himself by giving his readers civilized entertainment. . . . If he is a well-informed man and able to write decently, anything he writes about anything will divert his readers."

The eminent critic George Steiner once visited his Oxford adviser, the austere Humphry House, and on the don's lectern noticed a copy of his own recently printed Chancellor's English Prize essay. "I waited, I ached for some allusion to it. It came when I was already at the door. 'Ah yes, yes, your pamphlet. A touch dazzling, wouldn't you say?'" Steiner remarks that "the epithet fell like mid-winter."

When Franz Kafka submitted "The Metamorphosis" to the Berlin newspaper *Neue Rundschau,* one of its editors—the novelist Robert Musil, no less—asked him to cut the novella by a third.

Seventeen copies sold, of which eleven at trade price to free circulating libraries beyond the sea. Getting known . . . [pause] . . . Never knew such silence. The earth might be uninhabited.
—Samuel Beckett (*Krapp's Last Tape*)

It does seem to me that critics and reviewers can be loosely divided into two camps: Those who never let you forget that they are judge, jury, and, if need be, executioner; and those who humble themselves before a poem or novel, waiting for it to reveal its secrets to them. The first kind of critic aims to absorb the book; the second hopes to be absorbed by it.

In general, the macho critic is more fun to read. He (or she) is opinionated, controversial, argumentative, funny. Behind the showmanship, however, often lurks an ideologue's desire to persuade: This novelist is too self-absorbed; that biography is pedestrian; those views are wrongheaded; these stories are wonderful. For such a self-confident intellect the measure of all books becomes ultimately the critic's own taste, imagination, and convictions.

The receptive critic, by contrast, presumes that the work under review is the measure. He tries to avoid preconceptions and instead make himself open to the book's argument or its particular magic. If such a critic finds a novel boring or strange or mystifying, he more often than not assumes that he has failed to understand it. Rather than pass summary judgment, this unassertive but sensitive reader prefers to present an author's work accurately and sympathetically, employing his own artistry, sometimes considerable, in the service of the book.

Of course, most practicing critics mix these two approaches, sometimes uneasily, hoping to balance argument with information, razzle-dazzle with reverence, all the while trying to avoid the pitfalls of both. The strong critic sometimes grows tendentious, supercilious, or holier-than-thou, and actually might be happier as an op-ed columnist. In his turn, the gentler critic can seem to possess no standards at all, to be one of those people who likes everything; he may even relax into a carpet-slippers-and-port literary essayist, dreamily relating the adventures of his sensitive soul among the masterpieces.

I have never met an author who admitted that people did not buy his book because it was dull.—Somerset Maugham

TOUCHSTONES

One never forgives a work of art that is general and vague.
—Steven Millhauser

He who writes carelessly confesses thereby at the very outset that he does not attach much importance to his own thoughts.
—Arthur Schopenhauer

I have been told that when the late Sir Edward Marsh, composing his memoir of Rupert Brooke, wrote "Rupert left Rugby in a blaze of glory," the poet's mother, a lady of firm character, changed "a blaze of glory" to "July."—F. L. Lucas

Every great story . . . must leave in the mind of the sensitive reader an intangible residuum of pleasure; a cadence, a quality of voice that is exclusively the writer's own, individual, unique.
—Willa Cather

The style of an author should be the image of his mind, but the choice and command of language is the fruit of exercise.
—Edward Gibbon

The structure of a play is always the story of how the birds came home to roost.—Arthur Miller

A poet looks at the world as a man looks at a woman.
—Wallace Stevens

Originality does not consist in saying what no one has ever said before, but in saying exactly what you think yourself.
—Leslie Stephen

When you want to touch the reader's heart, try to be colder.
—Anton Chekhov

Lightness, quickness, exactitude, visibility, and multiplicity
—Italo Calvino (the traits in writing that he most admired)

Treachery, unrequited love, bereavement, toothache, bad food, poverty, etc. must count for nothing the moment one picks up one's notebook.—W. H. Auden

Caress the details, the divine details. . . . What color was the bottle containing the arsenic with which Emma Bovary poisoned herself?—Vladimir Nabokov

It is reported that when Pericles spoke, the people said, "How well he speaks." But when Demosthenes spoke, the people said, "Let us march."

DOING IT WITH STYLE

"We like," said Thoreau, "that a sentence should read as if its author, had he held a plough instead of a pen, could have drawn a furrow deep and straight to the end." Yes, but literature also needs ornamentation and dazzle, a touch of the idiosyncratic and gonzo. Certainly Shaker plainness is best for most writing, but sometimes it's nice to get all dressed up and strut your stuff. Make it new and strange and musical and fun.

Examples of such flamboyance? Read the the prose of Robert Burton, Jeremy Taylor, and Edward Gibbon; the poetry of John Webster, Milton, and Wallace Stevens; the fiction of Joseph Conrad, Ronald Firbank, Henry Green, John Updike, W. M. Spackman, William Gaddis; the essays of Walter Pater, Virginia Woolf, Ezra Pound, Edward Dahlberg, and William Gass; and the early journalism of Hunter Thompson. These writers' diction aims to astonish and seduce. Here Nicholson Baker, in his novel *Room Temperature*, defends old-fashioned punctuation:

> Such hybrids—of comma and parenthesis, or of semicolon and parenthesis, too—might at least in some cases allow for finer calibrations between phrases, subtler subordinations, irregular varieties of exuberance and magisteriality and fragile conjunction. In our desire for provincial correctness and holy-sounding simplicity and the rapid teachability of intern copy editors we had illegalized all variant forms—and, as with the loss of subvarieties of corn or apples, this homogenization of product was accomplished at a major unforeseen cost: our stiff-jointed prose was less able . . . to adapt itself to those very novelties of social and technological life whose careful interpretation and weight was the principal reason for the continued indispensability of the longer sentence.

William Gass even more exuberantly calls for colorful language at the conclusion of his novella *Willie Master's Lonesome Wife*:

> Let us have a language worthy of our world, a democratic style where rich and well-born nouns can roister with some sluttish verb yet find themselves content and uncomplained of. We want a diction which contains the quaint, the rare, the technical, the obsolete, the old, the lent, the nonce, the local slang and argot of the street, in neighborly confinement. Our tone should suit our time: uncommon quiet dashed with common thunder. It should be young and quick and sweet and dangerous as we are. Experimental

and expansive—venturesome enough to make the chemist envy and the physicist catch up—it will give new glasses to new eyes, and put those plots and patterns down we find our modern lot in. Metaphor must be its god now gods are metaphors.

And here is one-sentence marvel from Henry Green's *Concluding:* "At this instant, like a woman letting down her mass of hair from a white towel in which she had bound it, the sun came through for a moment, and lit the azaleas on either side before fog, redescending, blanketed these off again, as it might be white curtains, drawn by someone out of sight, over a palace bedroom window, to shut behind them a blonde princess undressing."

One may find similarly poetic rhythms even in writers thought to be as bluff and hearty as Rudyard Kipling: "She liked men and women, and she spoke of them—of kinglets she had known in the past, of her own youth and beauty, of the depredations of leopards and the eccentricities of Asiatic love" (*Kim*).

But no one excels Thomas Browne in baroque splendor, especially in "Urn Burial": "There is therfore some other hand that twines the thread of life than that of nature; wee are not onley ignorant in Antipathies and occult qualities, our ends are as obscure as our beginnings; the line of our dayes is drawne by night, and the various effects therein by a pencil that is invisible; wherein though wee confesse our ignorance, I am sure wee do not erre, if wee say, it is the hand of God."

The beauty of words, the sound and fall of sentences, a writer's distinctive voice rising from the page—these, in the end, provide the greatest and most lasting pleasures of a reading life.

Nine

MATTERS OF THE SPIRIT

Now on the field Ulysses stands alone,
The Greeks all fled, the Trojans pouring on;
But stands collected in himself and whole . . .

—ALEXANDER POPE

ANCIENT WAYS

Philosophy, wrote G. K. Chesterton, "is not the concern of those who pass through Divinity and Greats, but of those who pass through birth and death. If the ordinary man may not discuss existence, why should he be asked to conduct it?" At some point, nearly everyone agonizes over questions like: What kind of life will bring happiness or, at least, a sense of accomplishment and satisfaction? When faced with a moral dilemma—should I refuse to fight in an unjust war? should I be unfaithful to my spouse with this attractive and willing stranger?—how does one decide what to do? Are there ways to judge rightly the conflicting claims of duty and desire?

Most of the ancient Greek thinkers believed that one should aspire to a life of reason, and that *ataraxia*, a tranquil indifference to the world's vicissitudes, was the state of mind most worth cultivating. And yet it's hard not to wonder if untroubled serenity is really appropriate for human beings. Isn't there a point when too much self-mastery leads to a drying up of the inner self and the springs of sympathy? The early philosopher Heracleitus found strife to lie at the heart of all things; indeed, many people often feel most alive, most fulfilled, when they violate the dictates of conscience or even the promptings of their own self-interest. At least some of the time, guys want to be bad and women want to feel naughty. Perhaps a complete life should honor occasional acts of utter foolishness; otherwise, as Goya's nightmarish picture warns, "the dream of reason produces monsters."

In his first book, *The Birth of Tragedy*, Nietzsche argued that much of ancient culture actually grew out of a tension between Dionysiac passion and Apollonian reason; E. R. Dodds, in his classic *The Greeks and the Irrational*, further probed the place of madness, myth, and religious belief among the early Hellenes. Now, we have adopted something of a middle course. "The Greeks," concludes the contemporary classicist James Davidson, "imposed few rules from outside, but felt a civic responsibility to manage all appetites, to train themselves to deal with them, without trying to conquer them absolutely." This seems about right, especially as Freud would certainly add that an overzealous sense of duty results

mainly in neurosis. We can never wholly suppress our desires—
they are part of who we are—and so we should work with (or
around) them: We are, after all, only human, all too human.

THE HUMANE IDEAL

Besides the Epicureans, who actually believed in mild, reasonable
pleasures, and the sterner Stoics, there was a third major philosophical strain among the Greeks: the Skeptics. Even in summary,
they seem particularly attractive to the paranoid contemporary
sensibility. Xeniades of Corinth said that nothing at all is true.
Anaxarchus compared everything he saw to stage-paintings, that
is, illusions. Can you sound more jadedly postmodern than that?
Etymologically, a skeptic is an "inquirer" or "searcher," one who
feels that the truth can be sought but never quite found. No fa-
natics in these ranks, then, and no true believers. The effects of
this philosophy of noncommitted inquiry were really felt centuries later, when early modern thinkers again argued for intellectual tolerance and suspicion of all dogma. This liberal ideal has
probably been most vividly expressed by the mid twentieth-
century philosopher and essayist Isaiah Berlin.

As a thinker Isaiah Berlin espoused a liberalism that he dubbed
"deeply and uniquely English," but one which anybody of any na-
tionality might usefully adopt. In "The Three Strands in My
Life," Berlin argues "that decent respect for others and the toleration of dissent is better than pride and a sense of national mis-
sion; that liberty may be incompatible with, and better than, too

much efficiency; that pluralism and untidiness are, to those who value freedom, better than the rigorous imposition of all embracing systems, no matter how rational and disinterested." As is clear by now, these are my own views too.

Throughout his writing Berlin repeatedly warns against system builders, monistic theorists, all those who claim to know how we should live. He himself spoke up for "negative liberty"—leaving men and women alone to act essentially as they wished. But reformers and zealots typically insist on "positive liberty," that people should be free to choose not what they want but what is "rational." Of course, if the working class, say, acts "irrationally," the ignorant proles obviously need to be guided and reeducated by supposedly wiser, far-seeing guardians.

Berlin will have none of such managerialism, which at heart denies people their right to moral sovereignty. Rather than abstractions and theories, he stresses "the revealed preferences of ordinary men and women." In particular, Berlin recognized that our inner natures aren't unified and our desires aren't always clear even to ourselves; we are in fact interior battlefields of contradictory impulses. We need to accept our dividedness, just as a good society is one that allows for differences, conflict, and opposition.

In particular, we need "less Messianic ardour, more enlightened scepticism, more toleration of idiosyncrasies." Better to live with irreconcilable desires and incompatible values than to succumb to the meretricious allure of some fanatical, unitary vision. As the great philosopher Immanuel Kant observed, in a phrase that Berlin made his own watchword: "Out of the crooked timber of humanity no straight thing was ever made."

IN MYSTERIOUS WAYS

Surprisingly, the Bible itself may be interpreted as a subtle endorsement for independence of mind. Consider the relationship of God to man in the Old Testament. Even though its books were composed at different times by various writers, one still finds that they depict a distant past when the Lord made himself known to his chosen people directly. He ambles around the garden with Adam and Eve, chats to Moses up on Sinai, engages in a bit of roughhousing with Jacob. Gradually, however, God's appearances become less frequent; miracles become smaller and more personal in scale; kings and prophets are set up as divine representatives. In the late book of Esther, the Lord isn't even mentioned by name. Yahweh has hidden his face.

During this period of the deity's withdrawal the Bible also shows us how human beings, once the sullen, rebellious children of the Lord, gradually grow up and start taking charge of themselves and their world. The birth of Christ itself emphasizes the growing power of humankind: Once God formed man in his own image; now he forms himself in man's image (remember too how Jesus always refers to himself as the "Son of Man"). God has left us, say theologians like Robert E. Friedman, so that we may stand on our own feet, and we must consequently learn to accept a certain spiritual loneliness. That does seem the natural human condition, one that we assuage through useful work, family and friends, community service, art. And, of course, through religion, for those with the gift of belief.

BODY AND SOUL

Through much of its history Christianity promoted the mortification of the body and the supreme importance of the soul. Chastity, continence, the Paulist doctrine that it was better to marry than to burn—from the beginning Christianity, like virtually all other religions, has turned madly about sexual questions. Matters only start to alter in the Renaissance, when an ethos of self-denial was replaced by one of showy self-fulfillment in art, politics, and war. After the Reformation the inner life of a sinner grew intensely important, requiring frequent examinations of conscience and a daily moral bookkeeping. As a result, the church's yoke of obedience to dogma gave way to the agonizing and unending dilemmas of personal choice.

Yet overall, during the first 1,500 years of the Christian era, the relationship between the spiritual and the corporeal might be crudely summed up as: "How shall I live my life on this Earth so that my soul will be saved?" For the orthodox, the answer rested on the belief or hope of an afterlife in heaven. Complexity arose when Christian thinkers tried to fathom just where the soul was located in the body, or just how the body and soul were linked. Ancient medicine suggested that "animal spirits" might function as "bridging media" between the two seeming opposites, while the Incarnation itself—God in Man or God as Man—made literally manifest the everlasting and apparently insoluble mystery of how the material and immaterial might become one.

In the seventeenth century, everything changed (see Roy

Porter's various books, especially *Flesh in the Age of Reason*). René Descartes claimed that "mind was what distinguished humans from all other earthly beings," going so far as to locate the soul in the pineal gland; Thomas Hobbes went drastically further and proposed that man was wholly physical and talk of the soul was simply vacuous or deceitful. Once the author of *Leviathan* discarded the spiritual, the entire supernatural realm went with it. Soon John Locke asserted that we learn everything through our senses (starting life as a tabula rasa, or blank slate) and that experience of the world was sufficient in itself to develop our sense of self. Locke's *Essay Concerning Human Understanding* (1690) promulgated the notion that individual identity was simply a kind of stream of consciousness. We would feel essentially ourselves, no matter what our physical form, if we maintained this "fine thread" of personal awareness.

As is true today, once belief in the existence of a soul withered away, health and long life became the new piety. The body itself was reconceived as a machine or an elaborate network of plumbing; as the eighteenth-century German philosopher, scientist, and aphorist Georg Lichtenberg noted, "Everything that matters in life flows through tubes." What counted was "generous input and unimpeded outflow." Stagnation was death.

Even more than Locke, David Hume got rid of any surviving remnants of "the ghost in the machine": The genial Scots philosopher maintained that when he looked within he found only a "flux of perceptions." Hume further urged—contra all Christian and classical thinking—that reason should bow to feeling, since emotions were the actual motive forces that determined how people behaved. At heart, pleasure alone counted, whether bodily or—better yet for this bachelor—intellectual. Many of Hume's notions influenced his friend Adam Smith, who in his moral theory of sentiments stressed that the glue holding society together was our ability to sympathize and identify with other human beings. That sounds about right.

GUIDANCE COUNSELORS

Throughout history moral essayists have sought to answer the basic question of how a person should live his or her life in this world. Here are some of the central books of that great tradition.

1. Job. This Old Testament book examines the central mystery of earthly suffering and the apparent indifference of God, without giving any clear-cut answer.
2. Ecclesiastes. All is vanity, saith the Preacher, in this most despondent—yet oddly comforting—book of the Bible.
3. Plato's dialogues, especially *Symposium*, *Apology*, and *Republic*. Socrates, the great questioner of the ancient world, explores love, the good life, and the ideal community.
4. The Gospels. Follow the example and teachings of Jesus Christ, love your neighbor as yourself, and there awaits for you a life beyond death.
5. Marcus Aurelius, *Meditations*. Be indifferent to earthly troubles and retreat mentally to an interior citadel, above life's disorder, uncertainty and sorrow.

6. Horace, *Odes*. Seize the day, and enjoy the passing moment to its fullest before the darkness closes overhead.

7. Saint Augustine, *Confessions*. The model for all spiritual autobiographies, a formidable thinker's journey toward God. "Our soul is troubled till it rests in Thee."

8. Cicero, selected writings and letters. In his dialogues with friends, this most civilized of all the Romans, and a model to humanists for centuries, quietly propounds a life of measure and learning. Happiness is a library in a garden.

9. Boethius, *The Consolation of Philosophy*. Imprisoned and awaiting execution, Boethius discusses life's purpose with Lady Philosophy. An immensely influential book, translated by King Alfred and Chaucer, among others.

10. Michel de Montaigne, *Essays*. His essays are works of interior exploration, laced with learning and common sense. The humanist skeptic's *"Que sais-je?"*—What do I know?—was his motto. "And on the loftiest throne in the world we are still sitting on our own rear."

11. Baldassare Castiglione, *The Book of the Courtier*. Courtly love hoped to produce flowers of chivalry, but the Renaissance really showed how a gentleman should comport himself in society.

12. Niccolò Machiavelli, *The Prince*. To succeed in this secular world neither holiness nor service to others counts so much as Realpolitik and the manipulation of man's essentially fallen and corrupt nature.

13. Blaise Pascal, *Pensées*. "The condition of humanity: inconstancy, weariness, and disquiet." "Man is but a reed, the weakest thing in nature, but he is a thinking reed."

14. John Bunyan, *The Pilgrim's Progress*. An allegory of Christian progress through a world of temptation and sin. "So he passed over, and all the trumpets sounded for him on the other side."

15. François, duc de La Rochefoucauld, *Maxims*. We are bottomless lakes of egotism, and society is built on lying to others and oneself. "One is nearly always bored by the people with whom one is not allowed to be bored."

16. James Boswell, *Life of Samuel Johnson* (and Johnson's own works). Avoid cant in all things, and practice Christian charity. "Must helpless man, in ignorance sedate / Roll darkling down the torrent of his fate?"

17. Marquis de Sade, *Writings*. The "Divine Marquis" laughed at traditional morality and insisted that we live for pleasure and sometimes for pain.

18. Mary Wollstonecraft, *A Vindication of the Rights of Woman*. A manifesto and a clarion call—women deserve equal entitlement with men and lives of their own.

19. Stendhal, *Intimate Writings*. Deeply perceptive and kind, passionate and tender, a man of the world who is also a man of heart.

20. Ralph Waldo Emerson, *Essays* and *Journals*. Pith and vinegar from an exemplary American thinker. "The loves of flint and iron are naturally a little rougher than those of the nightingale and the rose."

21. John Henry Newman, *The Idea of a University*. From a liberal education "a habit of mind is formed which lasts through life,

of which the attributes are freedom, equitableness, calmness, moderation, and wisdom."

22. Sigmund Freud, papers and case studies. Our interor selves are strange, elusive, and fundamentally childish, yet we must somehow live with them. Even when wrong, he cast light upon darkness.

23. Simone Weil, selected writings. About suffering she was never wrong. Arguably the most intelligent and unsettling French-woman of her generation, she relates an unflinching spiritual journey toward God and death.

24. C. G. Jung, selected writings. In dreams we glimpse the drama and secrets of our inner beings. Once past forty, says this great analyst of the crises and possibilities of middle age, a person has "a duty and a necessity to give serious attention to himself."

25. Albert Camus, *The Myth of Sisyphus*. In the mid-twentieth century, the existentialist Camus found in Sisyphus—condemned for eternity to roll a boulder up a hill, over and over again—an image of human life as absurd yet still allowing for the possibility of happiness.

This short list leaves out as much as it includes. Where's Epictetus? Schopenhauer? Readers will also want to look for the religious poems of George Herbert, Gerard Manley Hopkins, and T. S. Eliot, as well as the fiction of Dostoyevsky, Tolstoy, Conrad, and Proust, all of whom have much to say about life and our journey through it.

Ten

LAST THINGS

To God, the right kind of human life looks well-meant but incompetent. Zeal is more important than technique. —w. h. auden

THE LIGHT AND THE DARK

Old age is the most unexpected of all the things that happen to a man.—Leon Trotsky

A thousand ages in thy sight
Are like an evening gone,
Short as the watch that ends the night
Before the rising sun.

Time, like an ever-rolling stream,
Bears all its sons away;
They fly forgotten, as a dream
Dies at the opening day.
—Isaac Watts ("O God, Our Help in Ages Past")

The cradle rocks above an abyss, and common sense tells us that our existence is but a brief crack of light between two eternities of darkness.—Vladimir Nabokov

No sooner do men despair of living forever than they are disposed to act as though they were to exist for but a day.
—Alexis de Tocqueville

If people knew the story of their lives, how many would then elect to live them?—Cormac McCarthy

Everybody has got to die, but I have always believed an exception would be made in my case. Now what?
—William Saroyan (on his deathbed)

Perhaps we will die knowing all the things that there are to know in the world, but from then on, we will only be a thing. We came and were seen by the world. Now, the world will continue to be seen, but we will have become invisible.—E. M. Cioran

A man's soul is like
A train schedule
A precise and detailed schedule
Of trains that will never run again.
—Yehuda Amichai

We learn only in old age what happened to us in our youth.
—Goethe

Soon you will have forgotten the world, and the world will have forgotten you.—Marcus Aurelius

Tell them I have led a happy life.—Ludwig Wittgenstein (last words)

But, Lord Crist! Whan that it remembreth me
Upon my yowthe, and my jolitee,
It tikleth me aboute myn herte roote.
Unto this day it dooth myn herte boote
That I have had my world as in my tyme.
—Chaucer (from "The Wife of Bath's Prologue")

The farce of dustiny.—James Joyce

TAKING CARE OF BUSINESS

1. Exercise. You don't need to become a bodybuilder or super-model, but do try to run, swim, lift weights, do yoga. To hear a

friend call out "Lookin' good" will brighten anyone's mood. *"Mens sano in corpore sano"*—a strong mind in a strong body—is as worthy a motto as any.

2. Brush and floss. The young, especially, can hardly imagine the expense, pain, and trouble of dental care in later life.

3. Be cool. Find your own style. Discover the clothes that make you feel like a million bucks, whether it's a tailored suit or a pair of jeans and a black T-shirt. Being well dressed, a woman once told Ralph Waldo Emerson, conveys a sense of satisfaction that religion itself is powerless to bestow.

4. Dine well. "Good dinners," said the novelist William Makepeace Thackeray, "have been the greatest vehicles of benevolence since man began to eat." To converse with friends, share a meal, sip a glass of wine—there are few better moments in life. Just don't overdo it.

5. Keep some perspective. To think that there could be worse than, say, being afflicted with high blood pressure can reduce the shock of an unexpected medical report. The occasional bout of melancholy may be regarded as merely the changeable weather of the soul. Wait a few days, and the dark skies will clear.

6. Be prepared. We all possess what the poet Paul Eluard called *"le dur désir de durer"*—the strong desire to keep on going on. But things happen, and if we are in unbearable agony, we will

yearn for its cessation. The one help here is to plan ahead, make clear your wishes about what should and should not be done for you if worse comes to worse. Because it might.

AND AFTER MANY A SUMMER

One day we will hear the oncologist say, "I'm afraid the prognosis is discouraging."—Donald Hall

One never knows, to paraphrase the opening sentence of Graham Greene's thriller *The Third Man,* just when or from where the blow will fall. But all of us recognize that adversity awaits each of us, sooner or later. C. S. Lewis called this the problem of pain, and the ancient philosophers, even the Stoics, agreed that pain was the chief obstacle to the serenity of heart and spirit that we should strive for during our lives.

When bad things happen to us, whether we are good people or not, we tend to lose at least some of our individuality, becoming yet another voice crying out to God or the universe: Why me? This isn't fair. How could this be happening? Isn't there anything to be done?

At such moments we find ourselves acting like little children, yearning for our mothers to make things better with a kiss or some words of comfort. As adults, we turn to our physicians or therapists and hope that they will assume that role and make the hurt go away. Sometimes they do; sometimes they don't.

What is most dispiriting is our fear, or even conviction, that because of illness or disaster we will become decrepit, machine-dependent, viewed as a medical case or a pariah, and eventually be cast aside by society and those we love. Most older people don't fear death so much as diminution, the loss of the self we have known most of our lives, the possibility that our minds and bodies will be taken from us and a dried husk left behind. We want so desperately to remain attractive and useful to the world. Cicero noted long ago that the unhappiest aspect of old age was feeling that people found one wearisome, a bore, irrelevant. Alas, no books offer a sure path through serious crisis. What works for you might not work for me, or for her, or for them. Still, reading can usually be a comfort, small but powerful.

Devout Christians have traditionally turned to the Bible or to heavenly minded thinkers for words of solace ("When all is done, human life is at the greatest and the best but like a froward child, that must be played with and humored a little to keep it quiet till it falls asleep."—William Temple). Others often read philosophers like Marcus Aurelius or Cicero, who ask us to rise above the corporeal and focus on our true self, the spirit. Buddhist scriptures remind us that were we truly to understand that the world is illusion and our desires only a source of suffering, we would be able to escape from this endless round of pain and continue our progress toward Nirvana. Nietzsche famously proclaimed that what doesn't destroy us can actually make us stronger. Sometimes a Wodehouse or Thurber might bring a smile, however wan.

Still, as Samuel Johnson movingly wrote, "the loss of our friends and companions impresses hourly upon us the necessity of our own departure; we know that the schemes of man are quickly at an end, that we must soon lie down in the grave with the for-gotten multitudes of former ages, and yield our place to others, who, like us, shall be driven awhile by hope or fear, about the surface of the earth, and then like us be lost in the shades of death."

Most of the time we find it simply inconceivable that we should not be. "We say," said Proust, "that the hour of death is uncertain, but when we say this we imagine that hour as situated in a vague and distant future. It never occurs to us that it has any relation to the day already begun or that death could come this very afternoon, which is anything but uncertain—this afternoon every hour of which is filled in advance."

In some dark hours it can help to think of all those who have come and gone before us. Not only parents and friends, but also the glorious dead, especially those who suffered more than we through what Alexander Pope called "this long disease, my life," or succumbed far too early: Keats, Shelley, and Rimbaud in their twenties; the composers Purcell and Mozart in their thirties; D. H. Lawrence and Scott Fitzgerald in their midforties; and so many others who were doing us some good. Those of us who live out our full term of three score and ten (or more) years ought to feel grateful. For after a certain distance, said Robert Louis Stevenson (who died at forty-four), with "every step we take in life we find the ice growing thinner below our feet, and all around us and behind us we see our contemporaries going through."

Art, poetry, music, philosophy, religion—these can console us, if our pain or despair isn't too great, or if we still hope that we might eventually get better. But if we won't get better, it may be harder to engage with anything beyond the fact of our pain and mortality. At such moments, one can take reliable comfort, even if never quite enough, from two sources: unconditional love from family and friends, and the knowledge that one has accomplished something good or useful in this life.

These are, in some senses, aspects of the same thing. We may be leaving this world—yet not entirely. Those who love us will remember us, talk of us, and keep alive our names. Not in any vainglorious way, but simply as a kind of thank-you for having been part of their own existences for a while, for having enriched their own lives. Similarly, to have given something of oneself to the world, even a small part of the world, makes us a part of it forever. Plato talked of this long ago in *The Symposium.* Children are the most obvious example of such giving, but they aren't the only ones. A teacher will have formed his or her pupils. To have created a garden or written a book, to have preserved a work of art from the destruction of time, to have helped the poor or the sick or the spiritually distressed, to have contributed to society more than one has taken—these are the sorts of triumphs available to any of us.

But there will always be regret, of some sort. How could there not be? In mid-career, the Russian short-story writer Isaac Babel was arrested by the secret police and never seen again. As he was hustled away, Babel was heard to shout, "But I was not given time to finish." Who is? Whatever you intend to accomplish with your life, you'd better get a move on, before that last call unexpectedly rings out, "Hurry up, please. It's time."

At the day of Judgment we shall not be asked what we have read but what we have done.—Thomas à Kempis

A SELECTIVE AND
IDIOSYNCRATIC WHO'S WHO

Several hundred writers, scholars and thinkers are quoted or mentioned in *Book by Book*. Most are fairly well known, and information about them may be readily found in standard reference books or online. But in some cases a name may hold a special significance (if just to me) or be only vaguely familiar to readers, and these I have chosen to briefly identify in the following pages. That said, virtually all the people and works I mention throughout *Book by Book* will reward whatever time you can give to them.

CHARLES ADDAMS (1912–1988). Celebrated *New Yorker* cartoonist, best known for his macabre humor. Creator of the originals for *The Addams Family*.

MORTIMER J. ADLER (1902–2001). Editor of *The Great Books of the Western World* and longtime advocate of serious reading.

JOAN AIKEN (1924–2004). Prolific writer for children, revered for her adventure-packed chronicles about the Cockney waif Dido Twite. Start with *The Wolves of Willoughby Chase*, though Dido first appears in *Black Hearts in Battersea*.

YEHUDA AMICHAI (1924–2000). Major Israeli poet, wistful and sensual in his themes, plain and matter-of-fact in his Hebrew.

WILLIAM ARROWSMITH (1924–1992). Teacher, classical scholar, and translator (of Petronius's *Satyricon* and much else).

MAX BEERBOHM (1872–1956). A dandy and self-confessed minor talent, "the Incomparable Max" is widely (and rightly) revered for his essays, stories, parodies, and drawings, these last mostly caricatures of his contemporaries.

E. F. BLEILER (b. 1920). Scholar, translator, and editor of genius, Bleiler rediscovered (and then published in Dover Books) many of the greatest works in the history of fantasy, detective fiction, horror, and science fiction.

LOUISE BROOKS (1906–1985). Silent screen star, and to many the ultimate vamp. Best known for *Pandora's Box*.

ITALO CALVINO (1923–1985). The major Italian writer of the 1960s and 1970s, playful and ingratiating, but always pushing against the limits of narrative form (see *If on a winter's night a traveler* and *Invisible Cities*).

GIROLAMO CARDANO (1501–1576). Renaissance mathematician and astrologer, and author of the strange and winning memoir *The Book of My Life*.

JOHN DICKSON CARR (1906–1977). The all-time master of the "locked-room mystery," in which a crime is committed under conditions that make it seem supernatural. (See *The Three Coffins* and *The Burning Court*.)

G. K. CHESTERTON (1874–1936). Journalist extraordinaire—and the creator of the second-greatest of all detectives, Father Brown, as well as the author of that inimitable, yet oft imitated, philosophical thriller, *The Man Who Was Thursday*.

E. M. CIORAN (1911–1995). Romanian-born essayist, long resident in Paris, famous for such morose but deeply intelligent books as *The Temptation to Exist* and *A Short History of Decay*.

KENNETH CLARK (1903–1983). Urbane and patrician, Clark was a leading figure in the British art establishment for much of his adult life and grew internationally famous through his television program *Civilisation*.

JOHN CLUTE (b. 1940). Arguably the major critic, scholar, and theorist of science fiction and fantasy of our time. See *The Encylopedia of Science Fiction* and *The Encyclopedia of Fantasy*.

COLETTE (1873–1954). Iconic Frenchwoman of letters; best known for her novels about love, especially *Chéri* and *Gigi*.

JOHN COLLIER (1850–1934). English short-story writer, long resident in Hollywood, specializing in tales of the macabre, most of them told in a breezy, Jazz-Age manner; see *Fancies and Goodnights*.

CYRIL CONNOLLY (1903–1974). Moody introspective English man of letters; celebrated for his wit, prose style, and hedonism.

PETER CONRAD (b. 1948). Wide-ranging twentieth-century scholar of English literature, modernism in all its forms, and opera.

K. C. CONSTANTINE (b. 1934). Author of a series of crime novels—starting with *The Rocksburg Railroad Murders*—set in a decaying, Pennsylvania steeltown. Wonderful depiction of working-class life.

ROBERT CRAFT (b. 1923). Conductor, astonishingly learned critic of art, music, and literature, secretary and assistant for many years to the composer Igor Stravinsky.

JOHN CROWLEY (b. 1942). American novelist, author (among other books) of *Little, Big*, often regarded as the finest American fantasy novel of our time.

EDWARD DAHLBERG (1900–1977). American novelist and essayist, master of a baroque, almost biblical prose style. His memoir of his mother, *Because I Was Flesh*, is an underrated masterpiece

GUY DAVENPORT (1927–2005). Encyclopedically learned American essayist (*The Geography of the Imagination*), translator and short-story writer (*Tatlin!*).

JAMES DAVIDSON (b. 1964). English scholar of antiquity; best known for *Fishcakes and Courtesans*, a study of self-control and the loss of such control in ancient Greek culture.

ROBERTSON DAVIES (1913–1995). Leading Canadian novelist; famous for his old-fashioned, highly theatrical personality. Key novels: *Fifth Business* and *What's Bred in the Bone*.

SUSAN DAVIS (1948–1999). American artist and illustrator, whose work often appeared in the *Washington Post* and the *New Yorker*.

LEO (b. 1933) and DIANE DILLON (b. 1933). Husband-and-wife team of artists; highly regarded for their distinctively bold and stylized illustrations for paperback covers and children's books.

DIOTIMA (ca. 400 B.C.). A probably fictional "wise woman" who instructed Socrates about the nature of love.

LORD DUNSANY (1878–1957). Irish writer, known for his luxuriant, poetic prose, vivid imagination, and masterly skill as a teller of fantastic tales. See *The Book of Wonder*.

UMBERTO ECO (b. 1932). Italian expert on semiotics (the study of linguistic and cultural signs) and author of such best-selling novels as *The Name of the Rose*.

WILLIAM EMPSON (1906–1984). Major influence on "New Criticism," largely through his early masterpiece *Seven Types of Ambiguity*, which appeared when he was in his midtwenties. An almost equally important English poet ("And learn a style from a despair").

RONALD FIRBANK (1886–1926). The archetypal "camp" novelist (*Concerning the Eccentricities of Cardinal Pirelli*), but also the genius who freed English prose from fustian heaviness and gave it lightness and air.

M. F. K. FISHER (1908–1992). Widely admired memoirist, writer on food, and celebrant of French life and culture—a sensual life related in sensuous prose.

ELLA FITZGERALD (1917–1996). The greatest all-round female jazz vocalist.

THEODOR FONTANE (1819–1898). Late-blossoming German writer, whose *Effi Briest*—about a young girl married to an incompatible older man—may be the finest German novel between Goethe's *Elective Affinities* and Thomas Mann's *Buddenbrooks*.

FORD MADOX FORD (1873–1939). The great pivot figure of modernism—a writer who personally knew Joseph Conrad and Henry James just as he later knew Ernest Hemingway and Ezra Pound. *The Good Soldier* has been called the finest "French" novel in English.

MICHEL FOUCAULT (1926–1984). Controversial (yet much revered) French philosopher and scholar, best known for his studies of repressive institutions and the history of sexuality.

CHARLES FOURIER (1772–1837). French Utopian socialist visionary, he theorized a society based on phalanxes, where people would lead lives of maximum freedom and self-expression.

KAREN JOY FOWLER (b. 1960). Highly original and genre-bending fantasy and science fiction writer (*Sarah Canary*). Author of the comic and touching novel, *The Jane Austen Book Club*.

NORTHROP FRYE (1912–1991). Canadian educator and critic, author of the masterpiece of the "archetypal" interpretation of literature, *Anatomy of Criticism*.

ANTHONY GRAFTON (b. 1950). Teacher and intellectual historian, specializing in Latin culture and learning during the Renaissance and early modern period.

HENRY GREEN (1905–1973). Author of nine slender novels, half with gerundive titles (*Living, Loving, Party Going*), all deeply admired by other writers (including John Updike and Eudora Welty).

DONALD HALL (b. 1928). Eminent poet, essayist, critic, interviewer (Pound, Eliot), teacher, and memoirist.

JAMES HAMILTON-PATERSON (b. 1941). Wide-ranging English writer, whose books include *Gerontius*, a Whitbread Prize–winning novel about the composer Edward Elgar, and a study of Ferdinand Marcos of the Philippines.

RUPERT HART-DAVIS (1907–1999). English publisher, biographer, and editor (of Oscar Wilde's letters). His correspondence with his Eton teacher, George Lyttelton, offers a panorama of London literary life during the late 1950s and early '60s.

ANTHONY HECHT (1923–2004). Eminent American poet, teacher, essayist and critic. A man of the most kindly sophistication and courtliness, he wrote verse known for its wit, formal perfection, and understated passion. Try *The Venetian Vespers*.

GEORGETTE HEYER (1902–1974). The modern mistress of the Regency romance. Her novels are built on wit, ingenuity, and moral complexity (see *A Civil Contract, Sprig Muslin*).

RICHARD HOFSTADTER (1916–1970). Social and intellectual historian, specializing in politics, and envied for his masterly and witty prose. *Anti-Intellectualism in American Life* remains one of the best books ever written about education in the nineteenth and twentieth centuries.

MICHAEL INNES (1906–1994). Pen name of Oxford professor J. I. M. Stewart, under which he produced extremely witty, donnish mysteries and imaginative spy thrillers. Most famous title: *Hamlet, Revenge!* but his greatest book is probably *Lament for a Maker*, his funniest *Appleby's End*.

DIANA WYNNE JONES (b. 1934). Major English writer of fantasy for children. Her books can range from hilarious to harrowing, and some—like *Hexwood*—are structurally highly complex. *Howl's Moving Castle* was made into a Japanese animated film.

HUGH KENNER (1923–2003). Important Canadian-American literary historian and critic, and the leading authority on twentieth-century modernism, able to marshal and connect the most disparate insights and facts. See *The Pound Era*.

SHERIDAN LE FANU (1814–1873). The leading Irish writer of ghost stories during the nineteenth century ("Green Tea," "Carmilla"), and author of *Uncle Silas*, a mystery novel as fine as *The Moonstone* or *The Woman in White*.

VERNON LEE (1856–1935). The penname of Violet Paget, an expert on Italian places, gardens, and history, who wrote many essays and a handful of incomparable supernatural stories, in particular the hauntingly sexy "Amour Dure" and "Oke of Okehurst."

MICHAEL LEVEY (b. 1927). Cultivated English art historian, authority on Italian art of the Renaissance and on French eighteenth-century painting.

F. L. LUCAS (1894–1967). English essayist and scholar; author of a book about prose style and editor of a groundbreaking edition of John Webster's plays.

ANTONIO MACHADO (1875–1939). Widely regarded as the greatest Spanish poet of modern times.

JULIAN MACLAREN-ROSS (1912–1964). English novelist, short-story writer, memoirist, and charming, feckless, hard-drinking, money-cadging legend in his own time (and after).

JAMES MARSHALL (1942–1992). Major author-illustrator of children's books. His masterpiece is probably the multivolume saga of the hippos George and Martha.

CHINA MIÉVILLE (b. 1972). English writer of baroque literary fantasy, in the tradition of Mervyn Peake (q.v.), marked by colorful vocabulary and political commitment. See *Perdido Street Station*.

STEVEN MILLHAUSER (b. 1943). Novelist (*Edwin Mullhouse*, the Pulitzer Prize–winning *Martin Dressler*) and short-story writer, possessed of a supple, lyric prose style and a wistful, romantic imagination. See the collections *The Barnum Museum* and *Little Kingdoms*.

J. B. MORTON (1893–1969). English journalist and comic writer (often under the name "Beachcomber").

FERDINAND MOUNT (b. 1939). Novelist, political commentator, and former editor of the *Times Literary Supplement*.

MARVIN MUDRICK (1921–1986). Teacher, critic, and essayist. Regarded by many as the fiercest book reviewer since Randall Jarrell. "When the French get heavy, they make the Germans look like ballerinas."

PHYLLIS REYNOLDS NAYLOR (b. 1933). Prolific author of books for children and teenagers. Best known for the Newbery Award-winner *Shiloh*, about a boy, his dog, and moral decision making.

E. NESBIT (1858–1924). Creator of *The Bastables* and the "Five Children" (e.g., *Five Children and It*), she is a key figure in the development of the modern children's novel, and especially of that subgenre in which the fantastic overturns the lives of ordinary schoolkids.

THOMAS LOVE PEACOCK (1785–1866). Learned and witty nineteenth-century writer who satirized the literature, politics, and culture of his time in a series of lighthearted "conversation" novels set mainly in English country houses. *Nightmare Abbey* and *Gryll Grange* are perhaps the best known.

MERVYN PEAKE (1911–1968). With J. R. R. Tolkien and T. H. White, the third great English fantasy novelist of the century, as well as an equally important artist and illustrator. His trilogy, consisting of *Titus Groan*, *Gormenghast*, and *Titus Alone*, possesses a dark, bitter flavor all its own.

ROBERT PHELPS (b. 1922). American man of letters, best known for several books devoted to Colette (*Earthly Paradise* gathers her autobiographical writings) and for his friendship and advocacy of writers like his contemporaries James Salter, Richard Howard, and Ned Rorem and, from the previous generation, Louise Bogan, Glenway Wescott, and James Agee.

E. K. RAND (1871–1945). Intellectual historian of antiquity and early medieval Europe. Best known for his *Founders of the Middle Ages.*

SAX ROHMER (1883–1959). Popular novelist and creator of the insidious Dr. Fu Manchu.

DENIS DE ROUGEMONT (1906–1985). Swiss scholar whose studies of sexual passion and obsession have been widely influential, though his advocacy of marriage and Christian love have tended to be somewhat slighted.

ALAN RYAN (b. 1941). English scholar of political philosophy, especially interested in Bertrand Russell.

JAMES SCHUYLER (1923–1991). Particularly troubled member of the New York school of poets, and close friend to John Ashbery and Frank O'Hara. One of the most ingratiating lyric voices of our time: see *The Morning of the Poem.*

W. M. SPACKMAN (1905–1998). Author of four masterly, syntactically demanding novels about love, generally between cultivated older men and college-age women. The first, and most admired, bears an unforgettable title: *An Armful of Warm Girl.*

REX STOUT (1886–1975). Creator of the great stay-at-home detective, the enormously fat, orchid-loving Nero Wolfe. Stylish literate mystery writing at its finest, and atmospheric evocations of New York in the 1930s and '40s.

GOTTFRIED VON STRASSBURG (d. 1250). Building upon the (now) incomplete work of the French writers Thomas and Béroul, he produced the most complete and polished account (admittedly in German) of the immortal love story of Tristan and Isolde.

JEAN TOOMER (1894–1967). Author of one of the most admired of all African American novels, *Cane*, an important influence on Toni Morrison, among others.

CHRÉTIEN DE TROYES (second half of the twelfth century). The major French author of chivalric romances. The finest is probably *Yvain*.

FRANK M. TURNER (b. 1944). Professor of history at Yale, director of the Beinecke Rare Book and Manuscript Library, and a leading authority on Victorian culture.

KENNETH TYNAN (1927–1980). During the 1950s the major English theater critic, later author of superb profiles of "show people" like Mel Brooks, Johnny Carson, Tom Stoppard, and Louise Brooks.

MARINA WARNER (b. 1946). Novelist and authority on fairy tales, nursery rhymes, and other aspects of the popular imagination. Her masterpiece thus far is *From the Beast to the Blonde*.

WOLFRAM VON ESCHENBACH (d. 1220). Author of *Parzival*, the greatest Middle High German epic: the story of the quest for the Holy Grail.

P. G. WODEHOUSE (1881–1975). The preeminent English comic novelist of the twentieth century, author of nearly a hundred books over seventy years. Creator of Jeeves and Bertie Wooster.

MARY WOLLSTONECRAFT (1759–1797). Pioneering advocate for women's rights, wife of philospher-novelist William Godwin, mother of Mary Shelley (author of *Frankenstein*). She died too young.

FRANCES YATES (1899–1981). Leading historian of Renaissance magic, alchemy, and estoteric philosophy. Her *Art of Memory* describes the "memory palaces" that enabled users to learn by heart epic poems, the Bible, anything.

STEFAN ZWEIG (1881–1942). Viennese novelist, short-story writer ("The Royal Game"), and biographer. *The World of Yesterday* is a moving memoir. Committed suicide in despair at the collapse of the Austro-Hungarian empire and the rise of Nazism.

ACKNOWLEDGMENTS

Above all, I want to thank librarians and booksellers everywhere: They have made *Book by Book* possible. As usual, Marian Peck Dirda and our three sons, Christopher, Michael, and Nathaniel, provided reality checks whenever I tended to drift off too long into bookish revery. McDaniel College, through the good graces of President Joan Coley, Provost Thomas Falkner, and Professor LeRoy Lad Panek (former chair of the English Department), provided me with a refuge in which to finish the initial drafts of my manuscript. Patricia and Allen Ahearn, owners of Quill and Brush Books, then allowed me to hole up in their back bedroom while I revised my text. At Writers Representatives, my agents, Glen Hartley and Lynn Chu, aided by their associates Catharine Sprinkel and Farah Peterson, first encouraged, then enthusiastically supported this project. Had I not had the good fortune to land a job at the *Washington Post Book World*, I would almost certainly have never been able to read so much or so widely during the past twenty-five and more years.

I would like to thank everyone at Henry Holt who helped make *Book by Book* a reality: in particular, John Sterling, Sadie Stein, Rita Quintas, and Annsley Rosner. Elvis Swift's chapter ornaments are as ingenious as they are delightful. Most of all, I wish to express my deepest gratitude to my editor, Vanessa Mobley, who encouraged me to think hard about everything I wrote, brought to each of these pages her own keen intelligence and taste, and in every way helped make this a better book.

All these people deserve a good deal of the credit for whatever merit *Book by Book* may possess. I alone am responsible for its mistakes, lacunae, and oversights.

ABOUT THE AUTHOR

MICHAEL DIRDA, a longtime columnist for the *Washington Post Book World,* received the 1993 Pulitzer Prize for criticism. He holds a Ph.D. in comparative literature from Cornell University and is the author of *Readings: Essays and Literary Entertainments,* the memoir *An Open Book,* and *Bound to Please,* a collection of biographical and critical essays about great writers and their work.